MONOGRAPH NO. 11 / 1974

The Seven Aspects of a General Map Projection

Thomas Wray

Surveys and Mapping Branch
Department of Energy, Mines and Resources
Ottawa, Canada

Supplement No. 2 to *Canadian Cartographer*, Vol. 11, 1974

*This monograph has been published with the help of a grant
from the National Research Council of Canada*

CARTOGRAPHICA

Published by B. V. Gutsell, Department of Geography
York University, Toronto, Canada

Printed in Canada
BY UNIVERSITY OF TORONTO PRESS

PREFACE

Three aspects (direct, transverse, oblique) are recognized for a conical (i.e. conic, cylindric, or azimuthal) map projection. The present work distinguishes seven aspects (direct, first transverse, second transverse, simple oblique, transverse oblique, skew, plagal) of a general map projection. For a conical projection the first transverse, the second transverse, and the transverse oblique aspects are indistinguishable and constitute the familiar transverse aspect, while the simple oblique, the skew, and the plagal aspects become the familiar oblique aspect.

The underlying mathematical idea in the analysis developed here is the symmetry group (or automorphism group) of the map projection. This idea, however, is kept implicit rather than made explicit to avoid burdening the reader with too many mathematical technicalities. Instead, the analysis is carried out in terms of the fundamental regions of these groups. These fundamental regions are identified in a coordinate system called the metagraticule and the aspects are named according to the incidence of the geographic poles with the vertices and sides of a fundamental region. For the general map projection, a fundamental region is a trirectangular spherical triangle; however for certain families of projections this triangle is no longer fundamental, thus the fundamental regions for these projections have to be identified and compared with the trirectangular triangle, and new names have to be given to the aspects of these peculiar projections. The conical projections constitute one of these peculiar families.

Other interesting situations can occur. Inconsistencies may have to be resolved in assigning aspect names when a projection is simultaneously a member of two different families of projections, and when the conventions for naming the aspects differ in the two families.

It has been usual to attempt to force the traditional three aspects of a conical projection onto the non-conical projections. This has led to bizarre descriptions of some projections in the literature. A list is given of several indirect non-conical projections that have been described in the literature and their aspects are identified according to the sevenfold scheme.

The author thanks: Brigadier L.J. Harris, Mr T.A. Porter, and Mr L.M. Sebert for valuable discussions and helpful criticism of this monograph; Mrs L.J. Pollock for her expert typing of the manuscript; and Mr G.G. Shoup and Mr R.E. Jamieson for their assistance in preparing the diagrams.

Thomas Wray

CONTENTS

FIGURES

TABLES

"What's the good of Mercator's North Poles and Equators,
Tropics, Zones, and Meridian Lines?"
So the Bellman would cry: and the crew would reply
"They are merely conventional signs!"

[Dodgson, 1960, p. 278]

1.

INTRODUCTION

The names "direct" (or "normal"), "transverse", and "oblique" for aspects of map projections as defined by L.P. Lee [1943-4] are satisfactory only when applied to conical (comprising conic, cylindric, and azimuthal)[1] projections. Lee admits that "it is difficult to extend the definitions to cover the non-conical projections, but a simple convenient test is that the direct aspect is always the simplest mathematically". The present work provides an extension of the definitions to non-conical projections. Lee's difficulty arises from two counts. First there are in general seven distinct aspects, not just three. Secondly, Lee, along with other previous writers on the subject, distinguishes his aspects in terms of the orientation of the conical axis. In the language used below, he describes the orientation of the metagraticule in terms of the graticule. We shall see below that the inverse description — the orientation of the graticule in terms of the metagraticule — provides the proper analysis of the various aspects.

The present work has two main parts. The first, consisting of Sections 2—8, develops the basic mathematical analysis and defines the various aspects and aspect parameters. The second main part, Sections 9—15, describes the peculiarities of various families of projections with regard to the analysis of Sections 2—8. In Sections 2—15 the earth is assumed to be spherical. Section 16 is the extension to the spheroid of

1

the analysis of Sections 2—8. Section 17 is a catalogue of examples of indirect aspects of non-conical projections. An appendix follows the text; its notes are numbered to agree with the superscript numbers in the text and tables.

2.

THE DIRECT ASPECT

Lee's criterion of mathematical simplicity is somewhat elusive. Some projections do not have a unique simplest aspect. The most glaring example is the Littrow projection, three distinct aspects of which are equally simple mathematically, whereas the other aspects are much more complicated. If we take the standard[2] complex coordinate system on the sphere and let $s = \psi + i\omega$ and $z = x + iy$, where ψ is the isometric latitude, ω is the longitude, x is the map northing, and y is the easting, then the equations (i) $z = \sinh s$, (ii) $z = \tanh s$, (iii) $z = \operatorname{sech} s$ define three projections which can be shown to be three different aspects of the same projection, the Littrow projection. We should choose one of the three as the direct aspect, but which one? All three are equally simple. If we regard the Littrow projection as a member of the Von der Mühll family, then we should take aspect (i) as direct; if as a member of the Lagrange polyconic family, then aspect (ii) should be regarded as direct. Aspects (i) and (iii) (but strangely enough not (ii)) are given independent status as projections (numbers 189 and 191, respectively) in Maurer's catalogue [1935].[3] We are obliged to make an arbitrary choice. Littrow's name is traditionally attached to aspect (i); this, along with the useful retroazimuthal property of aspect (i) [Jackson, 1967-8; Reignier, 1957, p. 257], is sufficient ground for us to define (i) as the direct aspect. We shall return to a more detailed discussion of Littrow's projection in Section 12.

In the light of the above discussion of the Littrow projection Lee's criterion should be amended thus: the direct aspect of a projection should be taken as the one which is the simplest mathematically, if there is a unique simplest one; if not, an arbitrary (possibly even capricious) choice of direct aspect should be made among those aspects which are relatively simplest.

3

3.

THE GRATICULE AND THE METAGRATICULE

The *graticule* is the usual net of meridians and parallels, either on the sphere or on a map. The word "bimeridian" will be used to denote a complete great circle, one half of which is a meridian. A map projection, in its direct aspect, is specified by expressing the plane coordinates in terms of the graticule. Indirect aspects of a projection are defined by the same equations as the direct aspect, not in terms of the graticule, but rather in terms of a net similar to the graticule and displaced on the sphere with respect to the graticule. Such a displaced net is a *metagraticule*.

On the sphere, a metagraticule resembles the graticule in all respects except location — it *is* the graticule, but rotated to a different orientation.[4] The concepts of *metameridian, bimetameridian, metaparallel, metequator, metapole, metalatitude,* and *metalongitude* follow naturally, with obvious definitions.

On a map, the metagraticule is the underlying net on top of which the map is plotted.[5] The metameridians are the lines which would be the meridians and the metaparallels are the lines which would be the parallels if the aspect were direct. The metagraticule of a map is the same for every aspect of the projection — it forms, as it were, the invariant framework of the projection. The three basic great circles (the metequator, the prime bimetameridian, the ninetieth bimetameridian) of the metagraticules of some of the more common map projections are identified in Table 1. The *prime* metameridian is that one which is most convenient to measure metalongitudes from; if a projection has a metameridional axis of symmetry (a central metameridian[6]) then this central metameridian is naturally taken as prime.

A few more definitions prove useful. The *nodes* are the intersections of the equator with the metequator. If we move meteastwards

TABLE 1

The three basic great circles of the metagraticule for some common projections.

Projection	Metequator	Prime bimetameridian	Ninetieth bimetameridian
Any singly symmetric projection	—	Vertical axis of symmetry (central metameridian)	—
Any doubly symmetric projection	Horizontal axis of symmetry	Vertical axis of symmetry (central metameridian)	—
Any cylindric projection	Horizontal straight line	Set of pairs of vertical straight lines	Set of pairs of vertical straight lines
Any azimuthal projection	Circle	Diameter	Diameter perpendicular to prime metameridian
Any conic projection	Arc of circle	Set of pairs of radii	Set of pairs of radii
Mollweide	Major axis of bounding ellipse	Minor axis together with bounding ellipse	Circle on minor axis as diameter
Aitoff	As Mollweide	As Mollweide	Transcendental oval through metapoles
Hammer	As Mollweide	As Mollweide	Algebraic oval through metapoles
Sanson	Horizontal axis of symmetry	Vertical axis of symmetry together with pair of bounding sinusoids	Pair of sinusoids halfway to boundary
Littrow	Line segment between singularities	Line equidistant from singularities	The two outer portions of the line through the singularities

along the metequator, the *ascending* node is the one where we enter the northern hemisphere while the *descending* node is the one where we enter the southern hemisphere. The *panmeridian* is the great circle containing the poles and the metapoles. It is the only great circle which is simultaneously a bimeridian and a bimetameridian, and is equidistant from the two nodes.

4.

EULER ANGLES

The rotation of the net which transforms the graticule into the metagraticule may be broken down into three simple rotations of the sphere about easily defined axes. In this section we consider three nets — the graticule, the metagraticule, regarded as fixed but arbitrarily located with respect to the graticule, and a moving "graticule" whose coordinates and lines are indicated here by quotation marks. The initial position of this "graticule" coincides with the graticule and the final position with the metagraticule.

The first rotation, through an angle α (measured positive eastwards), is about the polar axis. This rotation moves the "prime meridian" away from the prime meridian (of the graticule) and puts it into coincidence with the half of the panmeridian which contains the metasouth metapole. The "longitudes" thus acquired by the metanorth and metasouth metapoles are $180°$ and $0°$, respectively.

The second rotation has the diameter joining the nodes as axis. The "prime meridian" is moved through an angle β along the panmeridian, in the anticlockwise direction as seen from the ascending node, until the "north pole" coincides with the metanorth metapole. We see that β may take any value between $0°$ and $180°$ since we recognize that the metanorth metapole may lie anywhere on the sphere, including the southern hemisphere.

The third rotation, through an angle γ (measured positive meteastwards), takes place about the metapolar axis. The "prime meridian" is moved away from the panmeridian and into coincidence with the prime metameridian.

The three *Euler angles*, α, β, γ, as defined above[7], give a complete description of the relative orientation of the graticule and the metagraticule. We notice that the longitude (positive eastwards) of the metanorth metapole is $\alpha \pm 180°$, that the latitude (positive northwards) of the metanorth metapole and the metalatitude (positive metanorth-wards) of the north pole are both $90° - \beta$, and that the metalongitude (positive meteastwards) of the north pole is $-\gamma$. We denote these three quantities by Λ, Φ, Ω, and summarize their properties in Table 2 and Figure 1.

If $\beta = 0°$ or $180°$ the angles α and γ each become indeterminate since all bimeridians are panmeridians. However the combination $\alpha + \gamma$ (if $\beta = 0°$; $\alpha - \gamma$ if $\beta = 180°$) remains determinate and in fact measures the longitude of the prime metameridian. The metalongitude of the

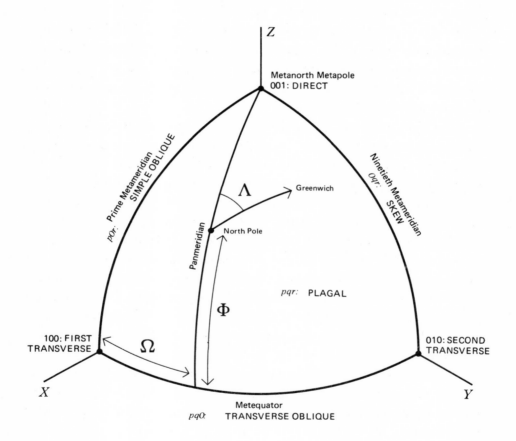

FIGURE 1. The fundamental trirectangular triangle; the cartesian frame *X, Y, Z;* the aspect parameters Λ, Φ, Ω; and the direction numbers and aspect names corresponding to different positions of the pole. By symmetry, only one of the eight trirectangular triangles need be shown.

TABLE 2

The aspect parameters Λ, Φ, Ω derived from the Euler angles.

First Euler angle	α	$\Lambda \pm 180°$
Longitude of metanorth metapole	$\alpha \pm 180°$	Λ
Longitude of metasouth metapole	α	$\Lambda \pm 180°$
Longitude of ascending node	$\alpha - 90°$	$\Lambda + 90°$
Longitude of descending node	$\alpha + 90°$	$\Lambda - 90°$
Metazimuth of prime meridian at north pole	$\alpha \pm 180°$	Λ
Second Euler angle	β	$90° - \Phi$
Latitude of metanorth metapole	$90° - \beta$	Φ
Latitude of metasouth metapole	$\beta - 90°$	$-\Phi$
Metalatitude of north pole	$90° - \beta$	Φ
Metalatitude of south pole	$\beta - 90°$	$-\Phi$
Third Euler angle	γ	$-\Omega$
Metalongitude of north pole	$-\gamma$	Ω
Metalongitude of south pole	$180° - \gamma$	$\Omega \pm 180°$
Metalongitude of ascending node	$270° - \gamma$	$\Omega - 90°$
Metalongitude of descending node	$90° - \gamma$	$\Omega + 90°$
Azimuth of prime metameridian at metanorth metapole	$-\gamma$	Ω

prime meridian is $-\alpha - \gamma$ if $\beta = 0°$ and $\alpha - \gamma$ if $\beta = 180°$. The quantities Λ and Ω (again defined as $\alpha \pm 180°$ and $-\gamma$ respectively) also become *individually* indeterminate if $\beta = 0°$ or $180°$ ($\Phi = \pm 90°$). If $\Phi = + 90°$, the combination $\Lambda - \Omega$ is the longitude of the hundred and eightieth metameridian and $\Omega - \Lambda$ is the metalongitude of the hundred and eightieth meridian, while if $\Phi = -90°$, $\Lambda + \Omega$ is the longitude of the hundred and eightieth metameridian and also the metalongitude of the hundred and eightieth meridian.

5.

THE PARAMETERS Λ, Φ, Ω

The graticule and the metagraticule are completely defined in terms of each other by means of the parameters Λ, Φ, Ω, which we shall now use in preference to the Euler angles α, β, γ. Any indirect aspect of a projection may be exactly specified by these three parameters. However if we want to assign *names* to aspects we have irrelevant information. The graticule has rotational symmetry about the polar axis; all meridians are exactly alike, and it does not matter which one is chosen to be the prime meridian — the usual choice of the Greenwich meridian is purely conventional. Hence the angle Λ (and of course α too) is, in principle, quite arbitrary. We may ignore it in the subsequent analysis. Of course on any particular map it is useful to specify it.

We are thus left with Φ and Ω, the metalatitude and metalongitude of the north pole. We cannot, in general, ignore Ω as we ignore Λ — a projection usually has a preferred metameridian which it is natural to take as the prime metameridian. However, for conical projections we *can* ignore Ω, since a cone (including the limiting cases of cylinder and plane) has rotational symmetry about its axis, corresponding to the metapolar axis. This immediately explains why the three aspects (direct, transverse, oblique) which are sufficient for conical projections become insufficient for general projections — they are defined in terms of Φ only (direct: $\Phi = \pm 90°$; transverse: $\Phi = 0°$; oblique: $\Phi \neq 0°, \pm 90°$) instead of Φ *and* Ω. We note that the pair (Φ, Ω) are *meta*coordinates of a point of the *graticule;* in other words our analysis of aspects depends on the orientation of the graticule in terms of the metagraticule, as promised in Section 1. The alternative interpretation of Φ as the latitude of the metanorth metapole and Ω as the azimuth of the prime metameridian at the metanorth metapole (cf. Table 2) is less symmetrical and is harder to work with.

10

6.

DIRECTION NUMBERS

Consider now a cartesian frame of reference with origin at the centre of the sphere and with the planes of the metequator, of the prime metameridian, and of the ninetieth metameridian as the XY, XZ, and YZ coordinate planes respectively, as in Figure 1. If the radius of the sphere is taken to be unity the coordinates of the north pole, and thus the direction cosines of the polar axis, are (cos Φ cos Ω, cos Φ sin Ω, sin Φ). A set of *direction ratios* is any triad of numbers p,q,r proportional (with positive factor) to the direction cosines. If no confusion results we may omit the commas and write pqr. The direction ratios satisfy a homogeneity relation: p,q,r and ps,qs,rs, where $s > 0$, represent the same direction. We shall use this homogeneity condition to simplify, for example, ppr to $1, 1, r/p$, provided, of course, that $p > 0$.

Unsigned[8] *direction numbers* are triads obtained from direction ratios by making all three signs positive. By using unsigned direction numbers we can conveniently ignore the metanorth-metasouth, the meteast-metawest, and the metanear-metafar[9] distinctions on the metagraticule and in the cartesian reference system.[10] This convention of ignoring signs gives the *same* direction numbers to both the north and south poles.[11] Unsigned direction numbers of course satisfy the homogeneity relation stated above for direction ratios, but now there is no need to check that the homogeneity factor is positive.

The chief advantages in using the direction numbers p,q,r as coordinates on the sphere auxiliary to the angles Φ, Ω are: first, the three coordinates p,q,r appear symmetrically in the definition of direction numbers whereas the definition of Φ and Ω is unsymmetric in the two angles; secondly, there are no singular points on the sphere in the pqr coordinate system, while the metapoles are singularities in the

Φ, Ω system; thirdly, the *pqr* system treats the three cartesian axes symmetrically, while the Φ, Ω system gives special emphasis to the Z axis; and fourthly, analytical expressions tend to be considerably simplified when expressed in terms of p,q,r — for instance, a great circle has a linear equation (or parametrization) in terms of p,q,r, while the corresponding expression in terms of Φ, Ω involves trigonometric expressions (see Tables 11 and 14 for formulas expressed in both systems).

7.

THE SEVEN ASPECTS

We define these in terms of the metacoordinates (Φ, Ω) of the north pole.[12] Equally well, we may use direction ratios, or, since we shall be ignoring signs, unsigned direction numbers. We may also specify the aspects in terms of the incidence of the metequator, the prime bimetameridian, and the ninetieth bimetameridian with the equator and the bimeridians. The definitions are given in Table 3 and the aspects are illustrated for the Mollweide projection in Figures 2—8. It should be noted that the words "transverse" and "oblique" have in each instance a qualifying word. This enables the six indirect aspects to have names distinct from the names of the two indirect aspects of a conical projection, which are "transverse" and "oblique" unqualified.

The term "transverse oblique" has previously been used by Bartholomew [1958, legend to frontispiece] to denote an aspect of the Mollweide projection. Our use of this term agrees with his. "Normal" is traditionally used as a synonym for "direct". There is no reason not to continue this tradition. "Plagal" is from the Greek πλάγιος, *oblique* (cf. *plagal mode, plagal cadence* in music, *plagioclase* in mineralogy). "Scalene", from σκαληνός, *uneven, unequal,* is suggested as an evocative synonym for the etymologically more precise "plagal".

The first and second transverse aspects resemble the transverse aspect of a conical projection. Together with the direct aspect they form a triad, the triad of *orthogonal* aspects. In terms of the cartesian coordinate system defined above, they correspond to the polar axis coinciding with one of the coordinate axes: X for first transverse, Y for second transverse, Z for direct, as in Figure 1.

As noted in Section 2 there may not be a unique aspect for a specific projection which is mathematically simpler than all the others. If there is one, it is the direct aspect by definition. If not, we may still be able to find three aspects, forming an orthogonal triad, which are

TABLE 3
The seven aspects.

Aspect	Metequator	Prime bimetameridian	Ninetieth bimetameridian	Metacoordinates Φ, Ω of pole	Inclinations of polar axis to X, Y, Z axes	Direction numbers pqr
Direct (normal)	Equator	Bimeridian	Bimeridian	$90°$, indeterminate	$90°$, $90°$, $0°$	001
Simple oblique	——	Bimeridian	——	Φ, $0°$	Φ, $90°$, $90° - \Phi$	p0r
First transverse	Bimeridian	Bimeridian	Equator	$0°$, $0°$	$0°$, $90°$, $90°$	100
Transverse oblique	Bimeridian	——	Bimeridian	$0°$, Ω	Ω, $90° - \Omega$, $90°$	pq0
Second transverse	Bimeridian	Equator	Bimeridian	$0°$, $90°$	$90°$, $0°$, $90°$	010
Skew	——	——	Bimeridian	Φ, $90°$	$90°$, Φ, $90° - \Phi$	0qr
Plagal (scalene)	——	——	——	Φ, Ω	$\cos^{-1}(\cos\Phi\cos\Omega)$, $\cos^{-1}(\cos\Phi\sin\Omega)$, $90° - \Phi$	pqr

TABLE 4
The four equioblique subaspects.

Subaspect	Metacoordinates Φ, Ω of pole	Inclinations of polar axis to X, Y, Z axes	Direction numbers pqr
Simple equioblique	$45°$, $0°$	$45°$, $90°$, $45°$	101
Transverse equioblique	$0°$, $45°$	$45°$, $45°$, $90°$	110
Equiskew	$45°$, $90°$	$90°$, $45°$, $45°$	011
Equiplagal (equiscalene)	$35°\ 16'$, $45°$	$54°\ 44'$, $54°\ 44'$, $54°\ 44'$	111

14

each simpler than any nonorthogonal aspect. One of the orthogonal aspects may then be arbitrarily chosen as direct, as in the case of the Littrow projection.

It often happens that one family of projections may have a general rule for choosing the direct aspect from among the three orthogonal aspects while another family overlapping with the first has its own general rule, and that the two rules do not agree in the overlap. For projections common to both families we have to make some arbitrary assignment of priority of membership in the families. Again, the Littrow projection is a typical example, being a member of the Lagrange and Von der Mühll families. The decision made in Section 2 for this projection gives membership priority to the Von der Mühll family. We shall meet other examples in Sections 10–13. Another peculiarity is that the generally simplest aspect for a given family may not be the simplest aspect for a particular member of the family. The Hotine meridian projection [Hotine, 1947-8, § 19.4, pp. 67-68; Lee, 1961-2, p. 217] is a good example. One particular choice of the constant in this projection (or projection family, since there is one parameter apart from a scale factor) gives the *transverse* Mercator projection as a special case of the *direct* Hotine projection.

The simple and the transverse oblique aspects, the skew aspect, and the plagal (or scalene) aspect resemble the oblique aspect of a conical projection. The simple oblique, the transverse oblique, and the skew aspects constitute the triad of *diagonal* aspects. The polar axis lies in one of the coordinate planes if the aspect is diagonal: the XY plane for transverse oblique, XZ for simple oblique, YZ for skew, as in Figure 1. In the plagal aspect the polar axis is inclined to all three coordinate planes.

We may give another description of these seven aspects. The three basic great circles of the metagraticule (the metequator, the prime bimetameridian, the ninetieth bimetameridian) divide the sphere into eight congruent trirectangular spherical triangles. For a picture of this dissection of the sphere, see [Du Val, 1964, p. 21, top left diagram]. The three orthogonal aspects correspond to the north pole coinciding with a vertex of one of these triangles and the three diagonal aspects to the north pole lying on a side, while the plagal aspect has the pole in the interior of a triangle. The sequence *direct, simple oblique, first transverse, transverse oblique, second transverse, skew, direct* corresponds to the pole making a complete circuit of the perimeter of one of the eight triangles. See Figure 1. Such a triangle is a "fundamental region" for the aspects. More formally, we define a *fundamental region* for our aspects to be a region on the sphere in which all possible aspects are represented once and once only by pole positions, where we do not regard as distinct two aspects whose only difference is that the pole of one is the reflection of the pole of the other in one of the cartesian coordinate planes.

This analysis is valid for any projection. However, it can happen that, for some projections, several of the aspects may be indistinguishable from one another. If this happens we retain the name "fundamental region" for a region which contains the pole positions of a complete set of *distinct* aspects. In such a case, the trirectangular triangle of Figure 1 is subdivided into a number (which may be infinite) of congruent fundamental regions. Projections whose fundamental regions are only portions of trirectangular triangles are discussed in Sections 9, 13, and 14.

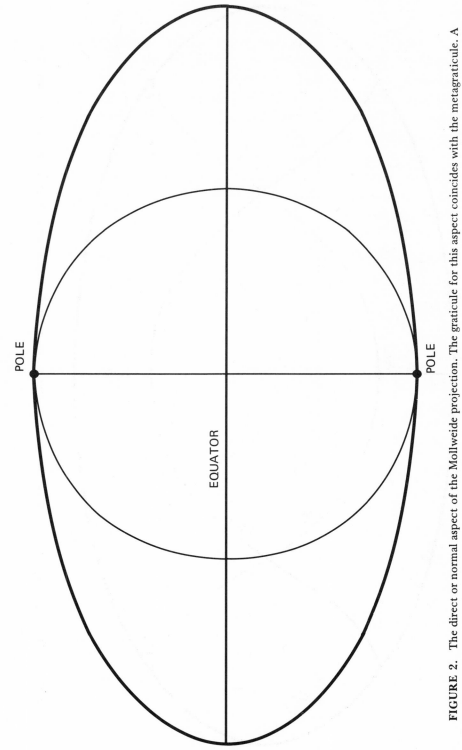

FIGURE 2. The direct or normal aspect of the Mollweide projection. The graticule for this aspect coincides with the metagraticule. A brief description of the metagraticule of this projection appears in Table 1.

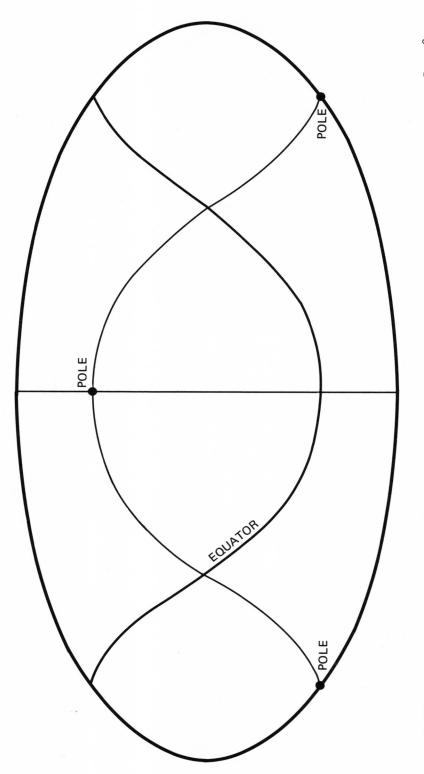

FIGURE 3. The simple oblique aspect of the Mollweide projection. The aspect illustrated here is the simple equioblique, with $\Phi = 45°$.

18

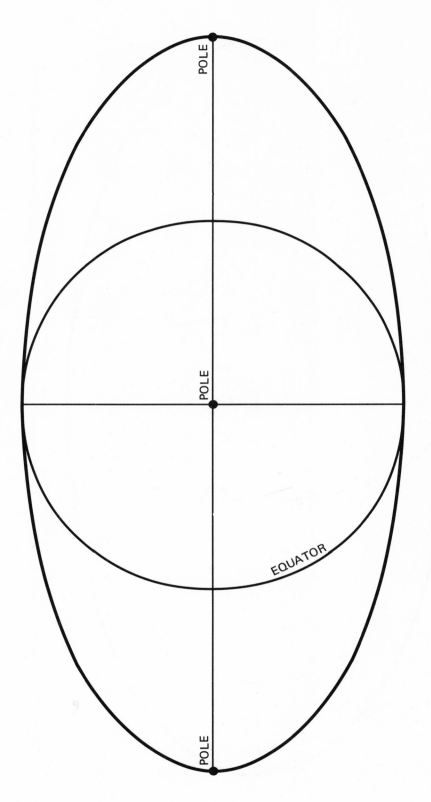

FIGURE 4. The first transverse aspect of the Mollweide projection.

19

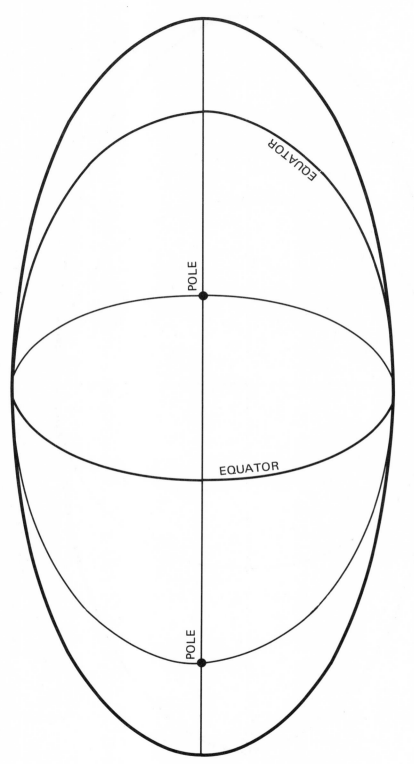

FIGURE 5. The transverse oblique aspect of the Mollweide projection. The aspect illustrated here is the transverse equioblique, with $\Omega = 45°$.

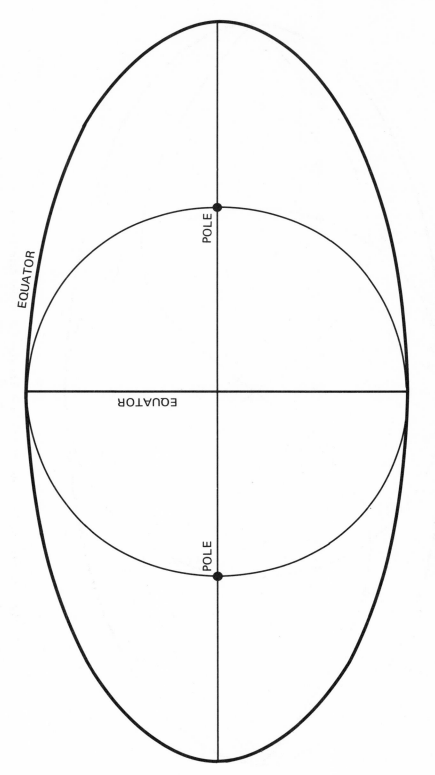

FIGURE 6. The second transverse aspect of the Mollweide projection.

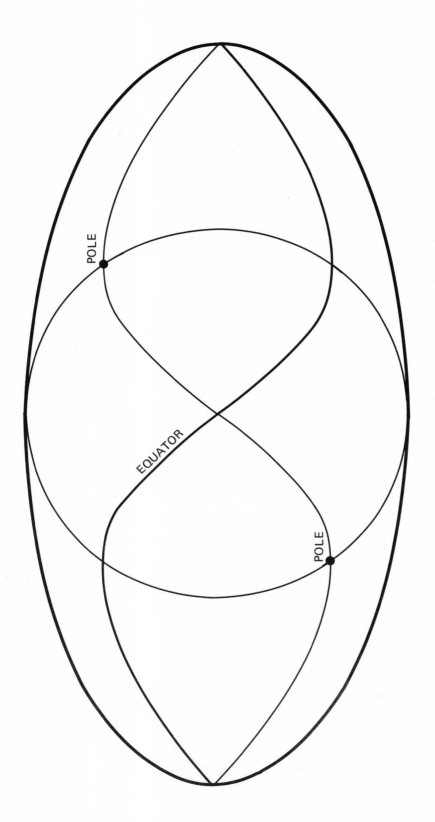

POLE

EQUATOR

POLE

FIGURE 7.   The skew aspect of the Mollweide projection. The aspect illustrated here is the equiskew, with $\Phi = 45°$.

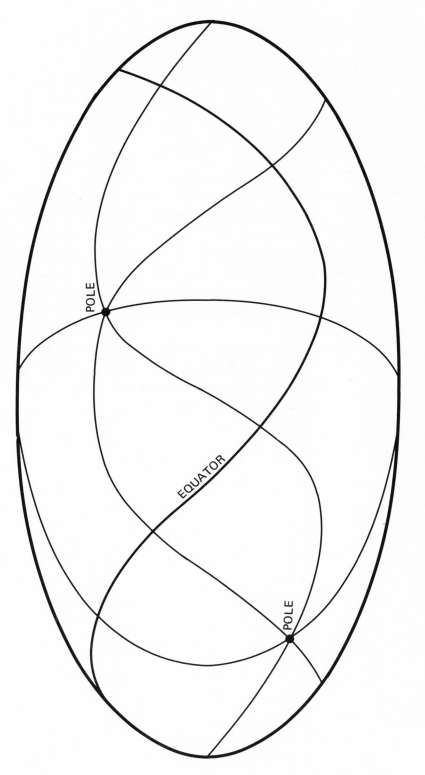

FIGURE 8. The plagal or scalene aspect of the Mollweide projection. The aspect illustrated here is the equiplagal or equiscalene, with $\Phi = 35°\ 16'$, $\Omega = 45°$.

8.

EQUIOBLIQUE SUBASPECTS

Each of the four nonorthogonal aspects possesses a special case ("subaspect") for which it is useful to have an independent name. The names and definitions are given in Table 4. The three equidiagonal subaspects arise when the polar axis makes angles of 45° with each of the two cartesian axes in whose plane it lies. The polar axis of the equiplagal (or equiscalene) subaspect makes equal angles with all three cartesian axes. A simple calculation yields $\sec^{-1}\sqrt{3} = 54°\ 44'$ for the size of each of these angles.

In terms of the eight trirectangular spherical triangles introduced in the previous section, the three equidiagonal subaspects have the pole at the midpoint of a side of a triangle while the equiplagal aspect has the pole at the centroid of one of the triangles.

9.

CONICAL PROJECTIONS

The definitions in Section 7 are applicable to any projection. However, as noted in Section 5, a cone (including the limiting cases of cylinder and plane) possesses rotational symmetry about its axis (corresponding to the metapolar axis). All metameridians are alike; we may choose any one of them as the prime metameridian. Equivalently, the angle Ω is completely arbitrary. The first transverse, second transverse, and transverse oblique aspects of a conical projection differ only in which generator of the cone is taken as the prime metameridian, and thus constitute a single *transverse* aspect. Similarly, the simple oblique, the skew, and the plagal aspects constitute a single *oblique* aspect. For example, the oblique Mercator map shown in [Steers, 1965, p. 155 and plate A facing p. 154; reprinted from Hinks, 1941, map A] can be considered to be simple oblique if either half of the panmeridian (152°E and 28°W) is taken as the prime metameridian; to be skew if the panmeridian is taken as the ninetieth bimetameridian (implying that the prime bimetameridian is the pair of generators through 0°N, 62°E and 0°N, 118°W); or to be plagal if any other generator is taken as prime. Again, if we take the origin of, say, a transverse Mercator map at the pole we may consider the aspect as first transverse; if, as is usually the case, at the intersection of the equator with the central meridian, as second transverse; while if the origin is taken elsewhere on the central meridian, we may regard the map as transverse oblique.

The word "equioblique", defined in the previous section, may conveniently be used for conical projections without a qualifying word: the *equioblique* aspect of a conical projection is the one for which $\Phi = 45°$. A word of caution — although the simple equioblique and the equiskew subaspects for a conical projection reduce to the (conical) equioblique, the transverse equioblique and the equiplagal subaspects do not. The transverse equioblique becomes transverse while the equiplagal becomes an oblique aspect with $\Phi = 35° 16'$.

The fundamental region for a conical projection collapses from a trirectangular spherical triangle to a great quadrant[13], a metameridian arc from the metapole to the metequator.

The considerations of this section apply to some projections with curved metameridians, such as the Wiechel [Close & George, 1952; Maurer, 1935, nr 53] and related projections [e.g. Maurer, 1935, nr 54-58]. Rotational symmetry (all metameridians alike) is sufficient for the collapse of the fundamental region to a great quadrant and for the seven aspects to reduce to three. The extra reflection symmetry of a conical projection and the straightness of its metameridians are irrelevant here.

10.

DOUBLY SYMMETRIC PROJECTIONS

These are projections with straight metequator and straight prime metameridian such that the metequator and the prime metameridian are axes of symmetry for the projection. The class includes the cylindric, pseudocylindric, and polyconic groups, among others.

It can be seen from Table 3 and from Figures 2 and 6 that the axes of symmetry in both the direct and second transverse aspects are the equator and a meridian. Both are "equatorial" aspects. The ambiguity discussed in Section 2 readily arises — given these two aspects of a doubly symmetric projection, which should be called direct, and which second transverse? Arbitrary choices are often necessary, and it has happened that the aspect which should be regarded as second transverse by the simplicity criterion has been given an independent name and been regarded as a direct projection in its own right. The cylindric projections, whose transverse aspect is usually coordinatized to agree with our definition of second transverse, are the prime example, with the Wetch projection (transverse cylindric "gnomonic"), the Cassini projection (transverse plate carrée), and the Gauss projection (or Lambert cylindric conformal: the transverse Mercator) all being named as projections. These three are properly transverse projections, and, since northings are usually measured from the equator, are best analyzed as second transverse. One rule of thumb that can be used for those projections in which one axis of symmetry represents a complete great circle while the other represents only half of a great circle is to choose as direct the aspect in which the complete great circle is the equator and the great semicircle is a meridian. This rule works not only for cylindric projections but also for the pseudocylindric, the polyconic, and other groups.

The first transverse aspect is a "polar" aspect. The pole is at the centre of the map (Figure 4) and a pair of bimeridians are the axes of symmetry. The simple oblique (Figure 3) and the transverse oblique (Figure 5) aspects are symmetrical about central meridians, the central meridian being the vertical[14] axis in the simple oblique and the horizontal axis in the transverse oblique. The skew aspect (Figure 7) has the poles symmetrically located with respect to the origin. The plagal aspect (Figure 8) is irregular. The three equidiagonal subaspects have the equator as the reflection of one of the bimeridians (the mirror for this reflection is the horizontal axis for the simple equioblique subaspect, the vertical axis for the transverse equioblique, and *either* axis for the equiskew [cf. Close, 1929; Steers, 1965, p. 172]).

Azimuthal projections may be regarded as doubly symmetric. However, the warning given in Section 7 applies here — the assignment of names to the aspects does not agree with the assignments when the projections are regarded as conical. The correlation of names is given in Table 5, which should be read, along with this paragraph, as an

TABLE 5

Aspects of azimuthal projections when regarded as doubly symmetric.

Aspect when regarded as doubly symmetric	Aspect when regarded as conical
Direct	Transverse (central meridian vertical)
First transverse	Direct
Second transverse	Transverse (central meridian horizontal)
Simple oblique	Oblique (central meridian vertical)
Transverse oblique	Oblique (central meridian horizontal)
Skew	Transverse (central meridian sloping)
Plagal	Oblique (central meridian sloping)

amplification of remarks made by Lee [1943-4, p. 196] about the stereographic and orthographic projections. It happens to be natural to take the "polar" aspect of an azimuthal projection as direct, treating the projection as conical, yet to regard the "polar" aspect of other doubly symmetric projections as first transverse. In case the reader is wondering about the cylindric projections, which are also simultaneously conical and doubly symmetric, there is no discrepancy in their naming, except of course for the simplifications made possible by ignoring Ω (Section 9).

One consequence of double symmetry is that the poles (in the direct aspect; metapoles in the general aspect) are alike. Either end of the metapolar axis may be chosen to be metanorth; in particular, the metanorth metapole may be chosen to lie in the northern hemisphere, or, if on the equator, then on the far[9] semicircle of the equator. In other words, for a general aspect of a doubly symmetric projection, we can always arrange that $\Phi \geqslant 0°$, and, if $\Phi = 0°$ (i.e. if the aspect is first transverse, transverse oblique, or second transverse), we may further arrange that $|\Lambda| \geqslant 90°$.

11.

SINGLY SYMMETRIC PROJECTIONS

In their direct (and most symmetrical) aspect these projections have a central meridian which is an axis of symmetry, without having any additional symmetries. The most familiar example is probably the Bonne projection. Hence in the general aspect these projections have a straight prime metameridian which is an axis of symmetry for the metagraticule.

The direct, the simple oblique, and the first transverse aspects all have central meridians as symmetry axes. The second transverse aspect has the equator as its symmetry axis. The other aspects are irregular.

A large number of projections may appear at first glance to be direct (or second transverse) aspects of a singly symmetric projection. However, a closer analysis can show extra hidden symmetries. For instance, the Briesemeister projection [Briesemeister, 1953; Steers, 1965, pp. 164-166] should not be considered as a direct singly symmetric projection, despite its being a named projection, but as a simple oblique doubly symmetric projection, whereas it is probably best to regard the Philbrick projection [Steers, 1965, pp. 202-204] as direct singly symmetric. Although this projection is based on a simple oblique uninterrupted Goode homolosine projection, which has a doubly symmetric metagraticule covering the whole sphere, Philbrick's interruptions destroy this double symmetry.

Projections whose only symmetry is equatorial may conveniently be regarded as second transverse aspects of singly symmetric projections.

12.

THE LAGRANGE POLYCONIC FAMILY AND THE VON DER MÜHLL FAMILY

In terms of the coordinate systems introduced in Section 2 these families are defined by the equations (i) $z = k \tanh (ns + c)$ and (ii) $z = k \sinh (ns + c)$ respectively. The real number k is a scale factor; useful choices are 1, $1/n$, $e^{\pm 2c}$. The "wedge constant" n is either a positive real or a pure imaginary number resembling the other cone constant. cone and c is a complex number resembling the other cone constant. The *proper* Lagrange and Von der Mühll families have n real; the *improper* families have n imaginary. The imaginary part of c is[15] $-n(\Lambda \pm \pi)$; for simplicity we shall measure longitudes from the central meridian thus making c real. The significance of the real part of c — or of c itself if we have put its imaginary part equal to zero — will be discussed shortly. The projections of both families are clearly conformal since (i) and (ii) express z as analytic functions of s.

The Lagrange projections, in their direct aspect (equation (i)) have circular[16] meridians and parallels. The Lagrange family, proper and improper, and including various limiting cases, is in fact the complete set of all those conformal projections which have all meridians and parallels circular in some aspect. The graticule (and hence the metagraticule since the aspect is direct) of a proper Lagrange projection is a mutually orthogonal pair of systems of coaxal circles, the meridian system being of the intersecting type with $z = \pm k$ as the intersection points and the parallel system being of the non-intersecting type with $z = \pm k$ as the limit points[17]. This graticule is geometrically like the graticule for the transverse stereographic projection (which is indeed a special case as we see below), the only difference being in the numbering of the meridians and the parallels. Conformality breaks down (except for $n = \frac{1}{2}$) at the singular points $z = \pm k$ where the wedge exponent[18] is $2n$. The parallel of isometric latitude $\psi = -c/n$, the "standard parallel"[19], is a straight line. If $c = 0$ this "standard parallel" is the equator and the projections are doubly symmetric; if $c \neq 0$ the parallels are renumbered and the double symmetry is lost — the projections are singly symmetric. The portion of the sphere which can be represented on the plane is bounded by the meridians $\pm 90°/n$; if $n \leqslant \frac{1}{2}$ the whole sphere can be represented.

The direct aspects (equation (ii)) of the proper Von der Mühll projections have hyperbolic meridians and elliptic parallels.[20] The graticule is a confocal system of conics with foci at $z = \pm ik$, the ellipses of the system being the parallels and the hyperbolas the meridians. The foci $z = \pm ik$ are singular points with wedge exponent $2n$. The "standard parallel" of isometric latitude $\psi = -c/n$ is a straight line; if $c = 0$ this parallel is the equator and the projections are doubly symmetric; if $c \neq 0$ the projections are only singly symmetric. Again, the portion of the sphere which can be represented on the plane is bounded by the meridians $\pm 90°/n$ and if $n \leqslant \frac{1}{2}$ the whole sphere (except for the poles) can be represented.

As noted above both families are singly symmetric whereas the two subfamilies obtained by putting $c = 0$ are doubly symmetric. If we set $k = e^{\pm 2c}$ in equation (i), shift the origin to $\pm k$, then let c tend to $\pm \infty$, the same sign being chosen in all three cases, the limiting case obtained of the Lagrange projection is the Lambert conformal conic projection, which has of course full conical symmetry.

The projections with interesting indirect aspects have $c = 0$ and $n = 0, \frac{1}{2}, 1$. Let $L(n)$ denote the Lagrange projection with $c = 0$ and a specific n, and $M(n)$ the corresponding Von der Mühll projection. If we put $k = 1/n$ in equations (i) and (ii), and let n tend to 0, we obtain $z = s$ as the common limit. Hence $L(0)$ and $M(0)$ are the same projection, the projection $z = s$, which is readily identified as the Mercator projection, whose aspects are the usual ones for a cylindric projection. The projection $L(\frac{1}{2})$ turns out to be the transverse stereographic projection. Since the aspects of $L(n)$ in general follow the rule for doubly symmetric projections, the correlation of aspect names in Table 5 is appropriate here.

The most interesting case is $n = 1$. A study of the behaviour of the projections $L(1)$ and $M(1)$ on the x and y axes, followed by an appeal to standard theorems on analytic continuation, readily yields the result that L(1) and M(1) are different aspects of the same projection, related in such a way that if either is regarded as direct the other is second transverse. For mainly historical reasons, as noted in Section 2, we choose M(1) as the direct aspect of this projection, the Littrow, and L(1) as the second transverse aspect. The rule of thumb given in Section 10 is of no use since both L(1) and M(1) map only great semicircles on their axes of symmetry. It is interesting to note that the overlap of the families L(n) and M(n) consists of two projections, corresponding to n = 0 and n = 1, and that the aspect naming rules for L(n) and M(n) agree for n = 0 but disagree for n = 1. The correlation of aspect names for the Littrow projection is shown in Table 6. The first transverse Littrow projection has the defining equation $z = k$ sech s.

TABLE 6

Correlation of aspect names for the Littrow projection regarded as a Lagrange and as a Von der Mühll projection. Our preferred identification is as a Von der Mühll projection.

Aspect when regarded as L(1)	Aspect when regarded as M(1)
Direct	Second transverse
First transverse	First transverse
Second transverse	Direct
Simple oblique	Transverse oblique
Transverse oblique	Simple oblique
Skew	Skew
Plagal	Plagal

If we add 90° to all our longitudes (i.e. put $\Lambda = -90°$, $c = i\pi/2$, or, alternatively, regard the ninetieth meridian west as prime) the three orthogonal aspects of the Littrow projection become $z = ik$ cosh s (direct), $z = -ik$ csch s (first transverse), $z = k$ coth s (second transverse). The factors $\pm i$ may be removed by trivial rotations of the map coordinate system through 90° and k can be put equal to 1. We thus see that the equation $z = f(s)$, where f is any one of the six standard hyperbolic trigonometric functions, defines the three orthogonal aspects of the Littrow projection, each hyperbolic function and its cofunction giving the same aspect. This result is summarized in Table 7.

TABLE 7

The three orthogonal aspects of the Littrow projection as given by the six hyperbolic functions.

Equation	Aspect
$z = \sinh s$	Direct
$z = \cosh s$	Direct (alternative)
$z = \tanh s$	Second transverse
$z = \coth s$	Second transverse (alternative)
$z = \operatorname{sech} s$	First transverse
$z = \operatorname{csch} s$	First transverse (alternative)

These alternative representations of the three orthogonal aspects by means of cofunctions arise essentially because the Littrow projection manages to pack half of each of the *three* basic great circles (metequator, prime bimetameridian, ninetieth bimetameridian) into the *two* coordinate axes of the map plane. We have, in each of the three aspects, two competing great semicircles for the role of central meridian. A similar but not so extreme situation arises for other projections, notably for the first transverse aspect of doubly symmetric projections, where both axes of symmetry represent bimeridians either of which may be taken as central.

Among the other Lagrange projections[21] we need only mention one. This is the projection $L(\frac{1}{4})$, Lagrange's conformal map of the whole sphere within a circle, which will be used in the next section.

13.

MODIFIED PROJECTIONS
—THE AITOFF-HAMMER AND
AUGUST-MILLER TRANSFORMATIONS

We discuss here two derived families of map projections to illustrate the point that the natural choice of aspect names for a derived projection need not agree with the choice of names for the parent projection.

The Aitoff-Hammer projections in their usual aspect are derived by applying the Aitoff-Hammer transformation to a transverse azimuthal projection. If the original transverse azimuthal projection is defined by $x = f(\phi,\omega)$, $y = g(\phi,\omega)$ where x = map northing, y = easting, ϕ = latitude, and ω = longitude measured from the central meridian, then the Aitoff-Hammer transformed projection is given by $x = f(\phi,n\omega)$, $ny = g(\phi,n\omega)$. Aitoff's projection is the transform of the Postel equidistant and Hammer's is the transform of the Lambert equiareal[22] projection; both have "wedge constant" $n = \frac{1}{2}$.

It seems natural to take the usual aspect as defined above as direct, thus the projections of the family are easily seen to be doubly symmetric. The Aitoff-Hammer transformation destroys the radial symmetry of the azimuthal projection, hence there is no point in taking a polar aspect as direct. The transformation involves compensating rescalings on the sphere and on the map (scaling factors n and $1/n$ respectively), parallel to the equator in both cases. Rescaling parallel to the central meridian is easily seen to give the second transverse aspect, while the polar aspect is first transverse. If we consider the rescaled direction as horizontal we see that the aspects of an Aitoff-Hammer projection agree with those of the original azimuthal projection regarded as doubly symmetric and are thus correlated with the (conical) aspects of the original azimuthal projection as in Table 5. Briesemeister's [1953; Steers, 1965, pp. 164-166] projection is best regarded as a simple equioblique Hammer projection with its eastings shrunk by one eighth.

The August-Miller projections are given in their most convenient aspect by the transformation $w = z + mz^3$ where $w = u + iv$, $u =$ northing, $v =$ easting, and z is the complex coordinate of a doubly symmetric Lagrange polyconic projection $L(n)$ — that is $z = \tanh ns$ where we have put $k = 1$ for convenience in the formula for $L(n)$. If m is a real constant we shall talk about the *restricted* August-Miller family, while for the *extended* August-Miller family we permit m to take complex values. If m is real and positive the transformation stretches the Lagrange graticule in the north-south direction and compresses it in the east-west direction. If m is real and negative the stretching is east-west and the compression is north-south. If m is permitted to be complex the elongation is along the straight line with bearing $-\frac{1}{2} \arg m$ through the centre of the map and the compression is in the perpendicular direction.

The type projections of the August-Miller family are (i) the August conformal projection within a nephroid[2][3], where $n = \frac{1}{4}$, $m = -\frac{1}{3}$, and (ii) the Miller modified stereographic projection for various values of m, where $n = \frac{1}{2}$. It is natural to give the August-Miller projections the same aspect names as the parent Lagrange projections. The restricted August-Miller projections are doubly symmetric; the direct aspects of the extended projections look very much like the skew aspects of doubly symmetric projections.

Nothing unusual happens unless $n = \frac{1}{2}$. If $n = \frac{1}{2}$ (the Miller modified stereographic projection) we find that allowing m to take complex values does not produce new projections but produces instead *indirect* aspects of projections with *real m*; the situation is even worse than this since, even for real m, the values m and $-m$ give two aspects of the same projection instead of different projections. It turns out, if we denote the August-Miller projection with parameters m, n by AM(m,n), that, in the case of m real and negative, the direct aspect of AM($m, \frac{1}{2}$) is the second transverse aspect of AM($|m|,\frac{1}{2}$), while, if m is complex, the direct AM($m,\frac{1}{2}$) is the skew AM($|m|,\frac{1}{2}$) with $\Phi = 90° - \frac{1}{2} \arg m$. The behaviour of the other aspects of AM($m,\frac{1}{2}$) is summarized in Table 8. What is happening is that the parent $L(\frac{1}{2})$ is the transverse stereographic projection and the radial symmetry of this projection effectively cancels out the extra degree of freedom obtained by

TABLE 8

Aspects of the Miller modified stereographic projection AM(m,1/2).

A. m real and positive

Aspect of AM(m,1/2)	Aspect of AM($|m|$,1/2)	Aspect of AM($-|m|$,1/2)
Direct	Direct	Second transverse
First transverse	First transverse	First transverse
Second transverse	Second transverse	Direct
Simple oblique	Simple oblique	Transverse oblique
Transverse oblique	Transverse oblique	Simple oblique
Skew	Skew	Skew
Plagal	Plagal	Plagal

B. m real and negative

Aspect of AM(m,1/2)	Aspect of AM($|m|$,1/2)	Aspect of AM($-|m|$,1/2)
Direct	Second transverse	Direct
First transverse	First transverse	First transverse
Second transverse	Direct	Second transverse
Simple oblique	Transverse oblique	Simple oblique
Transverse oblique	Simple oblique	Transverse oblique
Skew	Skew	Skew
Plagal	Plagal	Plagal

C. m complex, not real

Aspect of AM(m,1/2)	Aspect of AM($|m|$,1/2)	Aspect of AM($-|m|$,1/2)
Direct	Skew	Skew
First transverse	First transverse	First transverse
Second transverse	Skew	Skew
Simple oblique	Plagal	Plagal
Transverse oblique	Plagal	Plagal
Skew	Skew	Skew
Plagal	Plagal	Plagal

allowing m to take complex values. If we restrict m to real positive values (or in some work to real negative values for convenience) we have all seven aspects. For real m with arbitrary sign the second transverse and transverse oblique aspects (and half the cases of the skew and plagal aspects) lose their identity as individual aspects. The five remaining aspects remain distinct. There is no ambiguity if the first transverse aspect is now just called "transverse". If we permit complex m the seven aspects collapse to a mere three: first transverse; skew, including the limiting cases of direct and second transverse; and plagal, including the limiting cases of simple and transverse oblique. These are just the three aspects of the stereographic projection (Table 9; cf. Table 5), differently named.

TABLE 9

Correlation of aspect names between the extended Miller modified stereographic projection AM(m,1/2), m complex, and the original stereographic projection.

Aspect of AM(m,1/2)	Aspect of stereographic projection
First transverse	Direct
Skew (including limiting cases of direct and second transverse)	Transverse
Plagal (including limiting cases of simple and transverse oblique)	Oblique

We have the following choices open to us for the projections AM($m, \frac{1}{2}$):

(i) Restrict m to be real and positive. We have the full seven aspects.

(ii) Restrict m to be real and negative. Again we have all seven aspects, but differently named from (i). The correlation of names is given in Table 8A, B.

(iii) Restrict m to be real but of arbitrary sign. We have five distinct aspects as listed in Table 10.

(iv) Permit m to be complex. We have the three aspects listed in the first column of Table 9.

(v) Permit m to be complex and rename the three aspects to agree

TABLE 10

The five aspects of the restricted Miller modified stereographic projection
$AM(m,1/2)$, m real.

Aspect of $AM(|m|,1/2)$	Aspect of $AM(-|m|,1/2)$	Aspect of $AM(m,1/2)$
Direct	Second transverse	Direct
First transverse	First transverse	Transverse
Second transverse	Direct	Direct
Simple oblique	Transverse oblique	Oblique
Transverse oblique	Simple oblique	Oblique
Skew	Skew	Skew
Plagal	Plagal	Plagal

with those of the stereographic projection. The equation between (iv) and (v) is given by Table 9.

Each of the five choices has something to be said in its merit. Which choice is made should depend on the particular use to which the $AM(m, \frac{1}{2})$ projection is put.

We see that for the $AM(m, \frac{1}{2})$ projection there is an essential ambiguity even in the method of analysis to be used to distinguish the aspects. The difference between (i) and (ii) (or between (iv) and (v)) is of no more moment than the differences described in the remarks of Sections 2 and 12 concerning the Littrow projection, or the difference between Lee's [1943-4, p. 196] alternative descriptions of the stereographic and orthographic projections; but the difference between the three groups (i)-(ii), (iii), (iv)-(v), is much deeper. It should be noted that Miller [1953] tacitly assumes m to be real but says nothing about the sign.

Let us examine the five analyses in a little more detail. A fundamental region for analysis (i) and (ii) is a full trirectangular spherical triangle; for analysis (v) it is a great quadrant just as for the stereographic projection; for (iv) again a great quadrant, this time from the intersection of the metequator with the prime metameridian to the ninetieth bimetameridian. The spherical triangle with vertices at ($0°$ MN, $0°$ ME), ($90°$ MN), ($45°$ MN, $90°$ ME)[24] is a fundamental region for analysis (iii). This triangle is one half of a trirectangular triangle and itself has angles of $90°, 90°, 45°$ and sides $90°, 90°, 45°$. Its vertices (in direction numbers) are 001, 100, 011 and its sides are $p01$, $p11$, $0q1$. The triangle results from folding the half of the trirectangular triangle 001, 010, 100 which lies metasouth of the median $p11$ over to coincide with the metanorthern half. The vertex 010 is thus moved to 001, and the point $0qr$ (with $q > r$) is moved to $0rq$. In this way the transverse oblique and second transverse aspects lose their identity as distinct aspects. The fundamental triangle for (iii) may also be defined directly in terms of Φ and Ω by the inequalities $\Phi \geqslant 0°$, $0° \leqslant \Omega \leqslant 90°$, $\tan \Phi \geqslant \sin \Omega$. In the following section we shall see other examples of fundamental regions smaller than one of the eight large triangles but still larger than mere quadrant arcs.

14.

POLYHEDRAL AND DOUBLY PERIODIC PROJECTIONS

The most familiar example of a polyhedral projection is the gnomonic projection on a cube [Hinks, 1921b; Steers, 1965, pp. 49-52]. It is natural to take the aspect in which the pole is at the centre of a face as the direct aspect and to take the natural cartesian frame for the cube as the XYZ frame of Section 6. It is readily seen that there is only one distinct orthogonal aspect, since the first and second transverse aspects are indistinguishable from the direct. Equally, the three diagonal aspects (simple oblique, transverse oblique, skew) are indistinguishable from each other, while the equidiagonal subaspect (the pole at the midpoint of an edge) is distinct enough to deserve treatment as a special aspect. Similarly, the equiplagal, with the pole at the vertex of the cube, also deserves to be called an "aspect" rather than a subaspect.

The simplest way to see the fundamental regions is to divide a face of the cube in union-jack fashion into eight right-angled triangles. Any one of these eight triangles corresponds to a fundamental region on the sphere. The most convenient one of these fundamental regions is a right-angled spherical triangle with vertices (90° MN), (45° MN, 0° ME), (35° 16' MN, 45° ME) or 001, 101, 111 in direction numbers. Such a fundamental region is one sixth of one of the large trirectangular triangles of Section 7. The arrangement of fundamental regions on the sphere and on the cube is the arrangement of triangles shown by Du Val [1964, p. 19].

The three principal aspects occur when the pole coincides with a vertex of the fundamental region: 001 for orthogonal (i.e. direct), 101 for equidiagonal, and 111 for equiplagal. The three one-parameter aspects have the pole on one of the sides of the fundamental region: $p01$ when the pole is on a median of a cube face, $1q1$ when the pole lies on an edge of the cube, and $11r$ when the pole is on a diagonal of a face. The pole within the triangle gives the remaining two-parameter aspect. Thus we again have seven aspects, although these seven are not the seven defined in Section 7. Generally, the number of aspects of a projection depends on the shape of the fundamental region[25] — one aspect for each vertex, one for each side and one for the region itself. A triangular region will therefore always give seven aspects[26].

The vertices and edges of the fundamental regions for the cubic gnomonic projection may readily be characterized as the vertices and edges of the cube together with those of its reciprocal octahedron and of the associated semiregular polyhedra, the cuboctahedron and the rhombic dodecahedron [Coxeter, 1973, pp. 17-20, 25-26, 52; Holden, 1971, pp. 40-42, 50]. These vertices and edges are listed in Table 11. The description of the various aspects in terms of the pole coinciding with vertices or lying on edges of these four polyhedra is given in Tables 12 and 13.

Our initial requirements that the projection be gnomonic and the polyhedron a cube may be relaxed. The same analysis, with the same fundamental regions, holds for any polyhedron with cubic symmetry, in particular for the octahedron and the cuboctahedron. Du Val [1964, p. 19] shows the arrangement of fundamental regions on the octahedron as well as on the cube. The only requirement on the projection for the analysis to be valid is that the projection has to have cubic symmetry. In other words, the forty eight fundamental triangles should all be represented identically on the polyhedral map. This is the case, for example, in Fuller's dymaxion projection [Life, 1943] where the polyhedron is a cuboctahedron and the projection is chosen to give constant scale on each of the twenty four edges of the cuboctahedron. To ensure this, different plane projections are used for the square faces and for the triangular faces. Yet the fundamental regions (each consisting of one eighth of a square face together with one sixth of a triangular face) are all mapped congruently.

After cubic symmetry we study icosahedral symmetry. The two regular polyhedra with this symmetry are the icosahedron and the (pentagonal) dodecahedron, which are mutually reciprocal. The most symmetrical (and therefore mathematically simplest) arrangement of these polyhedra with respect to a rectangular cartesian coordinate system (which has cubic symmetry) is with the coordinate axes passing

TABLE 11

Vertices and edges of a mutually reciprocal cube and octahedron in their simplest orientation, together with the associated cuboctahedron and rhombic dodecahedron.

A. Vertices

Polyhedron	Unsigned direction numbers of vertex	Metacoordinates Φ, Ω of vertex
Cube	111	$35°\ 16'$, $45°$
Octahedron	100	$0°, 0°$
	010	$0°, 90°$
	001	$90°$, indeterminate
Cuboctahedron	011	$45°, 90°$
	101	$45°, 0°$
	110	$0°, 45°$

B. Edges

Polyhedron	Unsigned direction numbers of edge	Equation of edge
Cube	$*s11; 0 < s < 1$	$\tan \Phi = \sin \Omega,\ \Omega > 45°$
	$*1s1; 0 < s < 1$	$\tan \Phi = \cos \Omega,\ \Omega < 45°$
	$*11s; 0 < s < 1$	$\Omega = 45°, \qquad \Phi < 35°\ 16'$
Octahedron	$0qr$	$\Omega = 90°$
	$p0r$	$\Omega = 0°$
	$pq0$	$\Phi = 0°$
Rhombic	$s11; s > 1$	$\tan \Phi = \sin \Omega,\ \Omega < 45°$
dodecahedron	$1s1; s > 1$	$\tan \Phi = \cos \Omega,\ \Omega > 45°$
	$11s; s > 1$	$\Omega = 45°, \qquad \Phi > 35°\ 16'$

The starred edges are bisected by the coordinate planes; the expressions for these edges refer to half the edge only. Vertices and edges in the positive octant only $(0° \leqslant \Phi \leqslant 90°, 0° \leqslant \Omega \leqslant 90°)$ are given.

43

TABLE 12

Aspects of projections on a polyhedron with cubic symmetry.

Direction numbers of pole	Aspect
001	Octahedron vertex — "direct"
p01 where $p < 1$	Octahedron edge
101	Cuboctahedron vertex
1q1 where $q < 1$	Cube edge
111	Cube vertex
11r where $r > 1$	Rhombic dodecahedron edge
pqr, no two of p,q,r equal	Plagal

The fundamental triangle used in this table has vertices (90° MN), (45° MN, 0° ME), (35° 16′ MN, 45° ME).

TABLE 13

The aspects and subaspects of Tables 3, 4 on a polyhedron with cubic symmetry.

Aspect of Tables 3, 4	Direction numbers of pole	Aspect of Table 12
Direct	001	Octahedron vertex
First transverse	100	Octahedron vertex
Second transverse	010	Octahedron vertex
Simple oblique	p0r	Octahedron edge if $p = r$
Simple equioblique	101	Cuboctahedron vertex
Transverse oblique	pq0	Octahedron edge if $p = r$
Transverse equioblique	110	Cuboctahedron vertex
Skew	0qr	Octahedron edge if $q = r$
Equiskew	011	Cuboctahedron vertex
Plagal	pqr	Plagal if p,q,r are all different
Plagal	s11, 1s1, or 11s	Cube edge if $s < 1$; rhombic dodecahedron edge if $s > 1$
Equiplagal	111	Cube vertex

through the midpoint of an edge [Coxeter, 1973, p. 52; Du Val, 1964, pp. 27-29; Fejes Tóth, 1964, pp. 76, 105; Fisher, 1943, pp. 612-613; Gardner, 1961, pp. 91-92; Holden, 1971, pp. 32-33]. We need planes of reflection symmetry (see Section 6 and Appendix[10]), and, more importantly, three such planes which are mutually perpendicular. Taking diameters joining midpoints of edges (and not vertices, or centres of faces) as cartesian axes is the only way to ensure this.

The vertices and edges of the dodecahedron, icosahedron, and the associated icosidodecahedron and rhombic triacontahedron [Coxeter, 1973, pp. 17-20, 25-26, 52-53; Holden, 1971, pp. 40-42, 50] are given in Table 14. The constant τ is the famous "golden number" $\frac{1}{2} (1 + \sqrt{5})$, approximately 1.618 [Coxeter, 1961, ch. 11; Gardner, 1961, ch. 8]. This number satisfies the relations $\tau + 1 = \tau^2$ and $\tau - 1 = \tau^{-1}$. The

TABLE 14

Vertices and edges of a mutually reciprocal dodecahedron and icosahedron in their simplest orientation, together with the associated icosidodecahedron and rhombic triacontahedron.

A. Vertices

Polyhedron	Unsigned direction numbers of vertex	Metacoordinates Φ, Ω of vertex
Dodecahedron	111	35° 16′, 45°
	$01\tau^2$	69° 06′, 90°
	$\tau^2 01$	20° 54′, 0°
	$1\tau^2 0$	0°, 69° 06′
Icosahedron	$0\tau1$	31° 43′, 90°
	10τ	58° 17′, 0°
	$\tau10$	0°, 31° 43′
Icosidodecahedron	100	0°, 0°
	010	0°, 90°
	001	90°, indeterminate
	$1\tau\tau^2$	54°, 58° 17′
	$\tau^2 1\tau$	30°, 20° 54′
	$\tau\tau^2 1$	18°, 58° 17′

B. Edges

Polyhedron	Unsigned direction numbers of edge	Equation of edge	
Dodecahedron	*$01s$; $s>\tau+1$	$\Omega=90°$,	$\Phi>60°\ 06'$
	*$s01$; $s>\tau+1$	$\Omega=0°$,	$\Phi<20°\ 54'$
	*$1s0$; $s>\tau+1$	$\Phi=0°$,	$\Omega>69°\ 06'$
	$s-\tau, s-1, s$; $s>\tau$	$\tan\Phi=\tau^2\sin\Omega-\tau\cos\Omega$,	$\Omega>45°$
	$s-1, s, s-\tau$; $s>\tau$	$\tau\tan\Phi=\tau^2\cos\Omega-\sin\Omega$,	$\Omega>45°$
	$s, s-\tau, s-1$; $s>\tau$	$\tau^2\tan\Phi=\cos\Omega+\tau\sin\Omega$,	$\Omega<45°$
Icosahedron	*$01s$; $0<s<\tau-1$	$\Omega=90°$,	$\Phi<31°\ 43'$
	*$s01$; $0<s<\tau-1$	$\Omega=0°$,	$\Phi>58°\ 17'$
	*$1s0$; $0<s<\tau-1$	$\Phi=0°$,	$\Omega<31°\ 43'$
	$\tau-s, 1-s, s$; $0<s<1$	$\tan\Phi=\tau\cos\Omega-\tau^2\sin\Omega$	
	$1-s, s, \tau-s$; $0<s<1$	$\tau\tan\Phi=\tau^2\cos\Omega+\sin\Omega$	
	$s, \tau-s, 1-s$; $0<s<1$	$\tau^2\tan\Phi=\tau\sin\Omega-\cos\Omega$	
Rhombic triacontahedron	$01s$; $\tau-1<s<\tau+1$	$\Omega=90°$,	$31°\ 43'<\Phi<69°\ 06'$
	$s01$; $\tau-1<s<\tau+1$	$\Omega=0°$,	$20°\ 54'<\Phi<58°\ 17'$
	$1s0$; $\tau-1<s<\tau+1$	$\Phi=0°$,	$31°\ 43'<\Omega<69°\ 06'$
	$\tau+s, 1+s, s$; $s>0$	$\tan\Phi=\tau^2\sin\Omega-\tau\cos\Omega$,	$\Omega<45°$
	$1+s, s, \tau+s$; $s>0$	$\tau\tan\Phi=\tau^2\cos\Omega-\sin\Omega$,	$\Omega<45°$
	$s, \tau+s, 1+s$; $s>0$	$\tau^2\tan\Phi=\cos\Omega+\tau\sin\Omega$,	$\Omega>45°$
	$\tau+s, 1-s, s$; $0<s<1$	$\tau^2\tan\Phi=\cos\Omega-\tau\sin\Omega$	
	$1-s, s, \tau+s$; $0<s<1$	$\tan\Phi=\tau\cos\Omega+\tau^2\sin\Omega$	
	$s, \tau+s, 1-s$; $0<s<1$	$\tau\tan\Phi=\sin\Omega-\tau^2\cos\Omega$	

The starred edges are bisected by the coordinate planes; the expressions given for these edges refer to half the edge only. Vertices and edges in the positive octant only ($0°\leqslant\Phi\leqslant90°$, $0°\leqslant\Omega\leqslant90°$) are given.

hundred and twenty fundamental regions on each of the sphere, icosahedron, and dodecahedron are the triangles shown by Du Val [1964, p. 20]. The various aspects of map projections in terms of the incidence of the pole with the vertices and edges of the icosahedron, dodecahedron, icosidodecahedron, and rhombic triacontahedron are given in Tables 15 and 16. It should be noted in passing that the

TABLE 15

Non-plagal aspects of projections on a polyhedron with icosahedral symmetry.

Direction numbers of pole	Aspect
001	Icosidodecahedron vertex — "direct"
$10r$ where $r > \tau$	Icosahedron edge
10τ	Icosahedron vertex
$1 - s, s, \tau + s$ where $0 < s < 1$	Rhombic triacontahedron edge
$01\tau^2$	Dodecahedron vertex
$01r$ where $r > \tau^2$	Dodecahedron edge

The fundamental triangle used in this table has vertices ($90°$ MN), ($58°$ $17'$ MN, $0°$ ME), ($69°$ $06'$ MN, $90°$ ME).

icosahedron vertex aspect of Fisher [1943] is not a direct aspect — it is not the simplest mathematically.

Any polyhedron having icosahedral symmetry can have the same hundred and twenty fundamental regions defined on it. The only requirement on the projection for this analysis of aspects to be valid is that these hundred and twenty triangles be mapped congruently onto the polyhedron. Bradley's equiareal projection [Bradley, 1946] does not have this icosahedral symmetry, and is probably best analyzed as an interrupted doubly symmetric projection which happens to be drawn on an unfolded icosahedron.

The fifth of the convex regular polyhedra is the tetrahedron. Unlike the other four (cube, octahedron, dodecahedron, icosahedron) it is not centrally symmetric — each vertex is not opposite another vertex but opposite the centre of a face. Hence, if one pole on a tetrahedral map is at a vertex, the other pole will be at the centre of a face. Since we do not distinguish between the north and south poles in naming aspects (cf. Section 6 and Appendix[11]) we shall regard the pole-at-vertex aspect as the same aspect as the pole-at-face-centre aspect.

In a tetrahedral projection, the regions which should be mapped congruently are the triangles shown by Du Val [1964, p. 18]. These

TABLE 16

The aspects and subaspects of Tables 3, 4 on a polyhedron with icosahedral symmetry.

Aspect of Tables 3,4	Direction numbers of pole	Aspect of Table 15
Direct	001	Icosidodecahedron vertex
First transverse	100	Icosidodecahedron vertex
Second transverse	010	Icosidodecahedron vertex
Simple oblique	$p0r, p\tau < r$	Icosahedron edge
Simple oblique	$p0r, p\tau = r$	Icosahedron vertex
Simple oblique	$p0r, r/\tau < p < r\tau^2$	Rhombic triacontahedron edge
Simple oblique	$p0r, p = r\tau^2$	Dodecahedron vertex
Simple oblique	$p0r, p > r\tau^2$	Dodecahedron edge
Transverse oblique	$pq0, p > q\tau$	Icosahedron edge
Transverse oblique	$pq0, p = q\tau$	Icosahedron vertex
Transverse oblique	$pq0, p/\tau < q < p\tau^2$	Rhombic triacontahedron edge
Transverse oblique	$pq0, p\tau^2 = q$	Dodecahedron vertex
Transverse oblique	$pq0, p\tau^2 < q$	Dodecahedron edge
Skew	$0qr, q > r\tau$	Icosahedron edge
Skew	$0qr, q = r\tau$	Icosahedron vertex
Skew	$0qr, q/\tau < r < q\tau^2$	Rhombic triacontahedron edge
Skew	$0qr, q\tau^2 = r$	Dodecahedron vertex
Skew	$0qr, q\tau^2 < r$	Dodecahedron edge
Equiplagal	111	Dodecahedron vertex
Plagal	$1\tau\tau^2, \tau^2 1\tau$, or $\tau\tau^2 1$	Icosidodecahedron vertex
Plagal	pqr satisfying $p{:}q{:}r = \tau \pm s : 1 \pm s : \pm s$ or $p{:}q{:}r = 1 \pm s : \pm s : \tau \pm s$ or $p{:}q{:}r = \pm s : \tau \pm s : 1 \pm s$	Dodecahedron edge, icosahedron edge, or rhombic triacontahedron edge according to Table 14B
Plagal	Any other pqr	Plagal

triangles, however, are not fundamental regions for defining aspects. The reason is that a fundamental region has to be a subregion of one of the eight trirectangular spherical triangles of Section 7. We have therefore to combine the dissection of the sphere shown in [Du Val, 1964, p. 18] with the dissection shown in [Du Val, 1964, p. 21, top left diagram]. This combination is readily recognized as the dissection of [Du Val, 1964, p. 19], where the fundamental regions are identical with the cubic fundamental regions. The triangles which are mapped congruently on a tetrahedral projection thus consist of a pair of fundamental regions.

An alternative way of looking at the problem is to recognize that a cartesian frame defined by a metagraticule as in Section 6 automatically has cubic symmetry. The pattern of fundamental regions therefore has to have cubic symmetry as well as tetrahedral. The most symmetrical way to orient a tetrahedron with respect to a cube is with its vertices as alternate vertices of the cube and its edges as diagonals of faces of the cube [Coxeter, 1973, p. 52; Du Val, 1964, pp. 25-26; Holden, 1971, p. 29]. We take the natural cartesian frame of the cube as the cartesian frame of the metagraticule. The coordinate planes of this cartesian frame bisect the larger triangles of Du Val [1964, p. 18] into the smaller triangles of Du Val [1964, p. 19].

The description of the aspects of a tetrahedral projection, named in accordance with the rules for cubic symmetry, is given in Table 17.

The theory of doubly periodic projections is closely related to the theory of polyhedral projections in two distinct ways. First, any tetrahedral projection can be regarded as a doubly periodic projection by unfolding the tetrahedron into a triangle and using this triangle as the repeating element in a pattern covering the plane. L.P. Lee [1965] demonstrates this for his conformal tetrahedral projection, but his process is obviously applicable to any projection on a tetrahedron. It should be noted at this point that although the doubly periodic projections which have been described in the literature (for example, the projections due to Guyou, to Peirce, and to Adams) have all been derived using elliptic functions, and hence have been conformal, this requirement is quite unnecessary — it is quite simple to produce nonconformal doubly periodic projections, the simplest one resulting from Lee's unfolding-and-repeating technique applied to the tetrahedral gnomonic projection. Although any tetrahedral projection may be regarded as doubly periodic, the converse is not true.

The second relationship between doubly periodic projections and polyhedral projections is that the division of the plane implicit in a doubly periodic projection is quite analogous to the division of the sphere into regions to be mapped congruently in a polyhedral

TABLE 17

Aspects of a projection with tetrahedral symmetry named according to the rules for projections with cubic symmetry.

Aspect	Direction numbers of pole	Position of poles on tetrahedron
Octahedron vertex — "direct"	001, 010, or 100	Both at midpoints of edges.
Octahedron edge	$s01$, $1s0$, or $01s$	The poles each lie on a face and occupy identical positions on their respective faces.
Cuboctahedron vertex	011, 101, or 110	The poles each lie on a median of a face and occupy identical positions on their respective medians.
Cube edge	$s11$, $1s1$, or $11s$, where $s < 1$	Each on the portion of a median of a face between the centre of the face and a vertex.
Cube vertex	111	One pole at a vertex, the other at the centre of a face.
Rhombic dodecahedron edge	$s11$, $1s1$, or $11s$, where $s > 1$	One pole on an edge, the other on the portion of a median of a face between the centre of the face and a midpoint of an edge.
Plagal	pqr, no two of p,q,r equal	Any other position.

projection. These two types of division can be handled formally using very closely related mathematical ideas.[27] However we shall not explore the aspects of doubly periodic projections here owing to two practical difficulties which make that theory harder than the theory of polyhedral projections. The first is that instead of just three symmetry types[28] (cubic, icosahedral, and tetrahedral) there are now seventeen to consider [Coxeter, 1961, ch. 4; Fejes Tóth, 1964, pp. 21-40]. The second difficulty is that for several of these seventeen types the fundamental regions are no longer triangular but are four-sided.

15.

ASYMMETRIC PROJECTIONS

These are projections such as the Chamberlin trimetric which show no symmetry of the graticule in any aspect. No aspect is simpler[29] than another. We may certainly apply all the analysis of Sections 2-7, name one aspect arbitrarily as direct, choose some metameridian as prime, and define the various indirect aspects, but the exercise is pointless as no insight is gained into the structure of the projection. If all aspects are equally simple or equally complex there is no canonical one we should take as direct. The best solution is to list the various parameters for each map and to regard the projection for each map as a unique entity.

Of course, before doing this, we should check to make sure that there are no hidden symmetries. For example, if the base triangle of a Chamberlin projection happens to be isosceles then the projection has an axis of symmetry which can be taken as a prime metameridian and the projection can be analyzed as a singly symmetric projection. Another example — the polyhedric[30] projection, which used to be popular on the continent of Europe, appears at first sight to be as asymmetric as a Chamberlin projection. But closer examination shows it to be really an oblique orthographic, and hence azimuthal.

There are projections which are asymmetric overall but where the asymmetry is merely due to the projection being an asymmetric composite of maps each of which has a highly symmetric projection. Botley's octahedral gnomonic projection [Botley, 1953-4] is a good example which is best regarded as eight separate oblique gnomonic projections whose maps happen to be assembled into an irregular octahedron.

The existence of inherently asymmetric projections, such as the general case of the Chamberlin, should not be a cause of despair in the hope of classifying aspects. Although our analysis is impractical for these projections, in the sense that they cannot be reduced to simpler projections by rotating the sphere, there is nothing in the mathematics to make the analysis impossible or inapplicable — it is merely impractical.

If a projection has no symmetry, the analysis of Sections 2-8 is too fine a tool to use; it creates distinctions which do not really exist. Conversely, if a projection has too much symmetry (for example the various polyhedral and doubly periodic projections of Section 14), then the analysis of Sections 2-8 is a somewhat coarse tool — it fails to make distinctions that should be made. But, for the vast majority of those non-conical projections that are used in practice, the tool is of exactly the right fineness.

16.

EXTENSION TO THE SPHEROID

Up till now we have taken the earth to be a sphere. In this section we examine the analysis of aspects if the earth is spheroidal.

A spheroid, unlike a sphere, cannot be rotated through an arbitrary angle about an arbitrary axis through its centre and be expected to coincide with itself. Hence we cannot rotate the graticule as we have done for the sphere, and cannot define a metagraticule. The *a priori* problem — given a (direct) map projection, what is its (Λ, Φ, Ω)-aspect for a given Λ, Φ, Ω?– is not in general capable of solution. For four important classes of projection a solution can be given. This solution will be discussed later.

However, the *a posteriori* problem — given a map projection, find Λ, Φ, Ω such that the projection may be regarded as the (Λ, Φ, Ω)-aspect of a simpler projection (taken as the direct aspect) — is readily solvable. The trick is to take the equations of the given projection and of the direct projection and to set the eccentricity of the spheroid everywhere equal to zero in these equations. The new equations are thus equations of two projections of the sphere, and the parameters Λ, Φ, Ω relating these two new projections may be taken as the Λ, Φ, Ω of the original projection. In other words, we consider the given projection as a generalization to the spheroid of some projection of the sphere, we find the aspect parameters of the spherical projection and then we assign these aspect parameters to the original projection. This is the rationale behind ascribing the name "transverse Mercator" to Gauss's conformal projection of the spheroid with constant scale on a straight central meridian (sometimes called the Gauss-Krüger projection). On a sphere the corresponding projection is in fact the transverse $(\Phi = 0°)$ aspect of the Mercator projection.

There are two subtleties in this solution of the *a posteriori* problem. The first is that the parameters Φ and Ω do not in general have any obvious physical meaning on the spheroid. They are purely conventional. (A spheroid does possess an axis of rotational symmetry — the polar axis — so the Λ rotation makes sense.) The second subtlety is that the generalization of a projection from the sphere to the spheroid is not unique. As can be easily seen, an infinite number of distinct spheroidal projections can reduce to the same spherical projection when the eccentricity terms are put equal to zero. So the best that can be said is that the given projection is *one* of the (Λ, Φ, Ω)-aspects of the direct projection, rather than *the* (Λ, Φ, Ω)-aspect. This lack of uniqueness in generalizing a projection to the spheroid has been recognized by L.P. Lee[31] [1953-4; 1961-2, pp. 216-217] in the case of the "transverse Mercator".

Returning to the *a priori* problem, for certain classes of projection there are canonical transformations from the spheroid to the sphere which preserve the particular defining quality of the projection class. The sphere can then be mapped to the plane. These canonical transformations preserve the longitude unchanged but replace the latitude by an auxiliary spherical latitude. Four[32] such auxiliary latitudes are of use [Adams, 1921, pp. 12, 122, *et passim;* Deetz & Adams, 1944, p. 211; Lee, 1943-4, p. 198]: (i) the *conformal* latitude[33], the use of which maps the spheroid conformally to the sphere, (ii) the *authalic* or *equiareal* latitude, used to map the spheroid equiareally to the sphere, (iii) the *rectifying* latitude, used to map the meridians of the spheroid true to scale on the sphere, and (iv) the *parametric* or *reduced* latitude, which is defined by regarding the spheroid as obtained from a sphere by a uniform flattening perpendicular to the equatorial plane. The auxiliary spheres defined by these latitudes are the *conformal,* the *equiareal,* the *rectifying,* and the *reduced* spheres. Conformal projections of the spheroid may be defined as conformal projections of the conformal sphere; equiareal projections as equiareal projections of the equiareal sphere; penequidistant projections as equidistant projections of the rectifying sphere[34]; perspective projections as affine transforms of perspective projections of the reduced sphere [35].

We may define indirect aspects, complete with their parameters Λ, Φ, Ω, for these four classes of projection, by rotating the graticule to a metagraticule on the appropriate auxiliary sphere. Among the infinity of the aspects recognizable by the *a posteriori* approach as a (Λ, Φ, Ω)-aspect of a specific projection, one is singled out as canonical by this *a priori* approach using an auxiliary sphere, as long, of course, as the projection is in one of the four classes described in the previous paragraph — conformal, equiareal, penequidistant, or perspective[36]. This solution to the *a priori* problem for these four classes would indeed be an excellent one except for the embarrassing fact that well established names would have to be displaced. "*The* transverse Mercator projection", as defined by this solution, should be the Gauss-Schreiber, the projection obtained by taking the (spherical) transverse Mercator projection of the conformal sphere. But everyone understands the Gauss-Krüger, defined by constant scale on the central meridian, as the projection described by "*the* transverse Mercator projection of the spheroid". Similarly, "*the* transverse plate carrée projection of the spheroid" is the alternative name of the Cassini projection. Yet this is a true equidistant projection which is different from the penequidistant projection given by the transverse plate carrée of the rectifying sphere. Logically, these names should be displaced to that representative of the *a posteriori* set which can be regarded as most canonical, with good grounds for regarding the *a priori* solution as giving this canonical member — the important reasons being (i) that Λ, Φ, Ω now have physical interpretations on an auxiliary sphere, and (ii) mathematical simplicity. Thus "*the* (Λ, Φ, Ω)-aspect" would be the one given by the *a priori* solution while "*a* (Λ, Φ, Ω)-aspect" is any one of the *a posteriori* set which contains the *a priori* solution. But established practice, at least for the names "transverse Mercator" and "transverse plate carrée", is probably too strong to accept such a reform in terminology. However, there is no reason not to adopt it for other projections.

Unfortunately there seems to be no way to define a canonical *a priori* representative of the *a posteriori* set if the projection is not conformal, equiareal, penequidistant, nor perspective.

17.

A CATALOGUE OF VARIOUS ASPECTS OF NON-CONICAL PROJECTIONS

We conclude by listing various non-conical projections that have had indirect aspects described or drawn in the literature. The list, Table 18, is not meant to be exhaustive. There have doubtless been many indirect projections described that have not come to the author's attention.

Table 18 includes several direct aspects. The reason is twofold: firstly, to enable the reader to compare the indirect aspects with the direct aspect of the same projection; secondly, to provide a reference for projections where even the direct aspect may be unfamiliar to the reader.

The first column of Table 18 gives the projection; the second column the aspect. In the third column the parameters Λ, Φ, Ω are given for indirect projections and Φ, $\Lambda - \Omega$ for direct projections. Recall that while two parameters Φ, Ω are sufficient to *define* an aspect, three parameters Λ, Φ, Ω are necessary to *describe* the aspect of a specific map. (To refresh the reader's memory, Λ is the metazimuth of the prime meridian at the north pole and also the longitude of the metanorth metapole, Φ is the metalatitude of the north pole and also the latitude of the metanorth metapole, while Ω is the metalongitude of the north pole and also the azimuth of the prime metameridian at the metanorth metapole. North, east, metanorth, and meteast are taken to be the positive directions. If $\Phi = \pm 90°$ the aspect is direct, and Λ and Ω lose their separate identities. However, if $\Phi = +90°$, the difference $\Lambda - \Omega$ is the longitude of the hundred and eightieth metameridian, and $\Omega - \Lambda$ is the metalongitude of the hundred and eightieth meridian, while if $\Phi = -90°$, the sum $\Lambda + \Omega$ is the longitude of the hundred and eightieth metameridian and is also the metalongitude of the hundred and eightieth meridian.) It is readily seen from

Table 18 that the aspect names depend only on Φ and Ω; Λ may be quite arbitrary.

The convention given at the end of Section 10, for the choice of which end of the metapolar axis is to be called metanorth if the projection is doubly symmetric, has been adopted. The aspect parameters given for the various polyhedral projections are not unique owing to the high symmetry of the regular polyhedra — on a cube, for instance, there are six possible choices of metanorth metapole (the centre of any of the six faces).

The fourth column illustrates the rather chaotic and often inconsistent terminology that has grown up from the failure to recognize that a general map projection has seven qualitatively distinct aspects, not just three, that these seven aspects are quantitatively defined by two parameters, not just one, and that they are completely described by three parameters, not just two. Hinks [1921b] appears to be aware of the difficulty, but he goes no further than to distinguish "inclined" (*simple oblique* in the present work) from "oblique" (*plagal*).

TABLE 18

Catalogue of aspects of non-conical projections which have been described in the literature.

Projection	Aspect	Aspect parameters (Λ, Φ, Ω)	Name given in reference	Reference
1. Sanson	Direct	$\Phi = +90°$, $\Lambda - \Omega$ unspecified (meridians unnumbered)	"Equatorial"	Robinson & Sale, 1969, p. 215
2. Sanson	Simple oblique	(unspecified, $+30°$, $0°$)	"Oblique"	Robinson & Sale, 1969, p. 215
3. Sanson	First transverse	(unspecified, $0°$, $0°$)	"Polar"	Robinson & Sale, 1969, p. 215
4. Mollweide	Direct	$\Phi = +90°$, $\Lambda - \Omega = \pm180°$	"Mollweide's Projection", "Mollweide's Projection"	Steers, 1965, p. 169 Robinson & Sale, 1969, p. 228
5. Mollweide	Simple oblique	($\pm180°$, $+60°$, $0°$)	"Oblique Mollweide projection"	Robinson & Sale, 1969, p. 244
6. Mollweide	Transverse (equi)oblique	($-120°$, $0°$, $+45°$)	"The 'Atlantis' projection, a transverse oblique homolographic equal-area arrangement"	Bartholomew, 1958, frontispiece
7. Mollweide	Second transverse	($+160°$, $0°$, $-90°$)	"A transverse Mollweide, with major axis the meridian 70° E. – 110° W.", "The Transverse Mollweide"	Hinks, 1921a, frontispiece and p. 61 Steers, 1965, pp. 170-172

Projection	Aspect	Aspect parameters (Λ, Φ, Ω)	Name given in reference	Reference
8. Mollweide	(Equi)skew	$(+90°, +45°, -90°)$	"The oblique Mollweide Projection with pole transferred to the point 45° North 90° West of the Normal Projection"	Close, 1929
			"The Oblique Mollweide"	Steers, 1965, pp. 172-174
9. Hammer	Direct	$\Phi = +90°$, $\Lambda - \Omega = \pm180°$	"Hammer's Projection"	Steers, 1965, p. 162
			"Aitoff's equal area projection"	Deetz & Adams, 1945, plate V
10. Hammer	Simple oblique	$(+30°, +60°, 0°)$	"Oblique Aitoff Projection"	Lewis & Campbell, 1966, pp. 6, 7, 16
11. Hammer	Simple oblique	$(-150°, +60°, 0°)$	"Oblique Aitoff Projection"	Lewis & Campbell, 1966, pp. 6, 7, 16
12. Hammer	Simple (equi)oblique	$(\pm180°, +45°, 0°)$	"'Nordic' projection . . . an Oblique Area-true Projection . . ."	Bartholomew, 1958, plate 7
13. Hammer	Simple (equi)oblique	$(+15°, +45°, 0°)$	"'Nordic' projection, Centre 45° N.: 165° W."	Bartholomew, 1958, plate 7
14. Hammer	Simple (equi)oblique	$(-165°, +45°, 0°)$	"W. Briesemeister's development of the oblique form of Hammer's graticule"	Hall, 1948 Steers, 1965, p. 164
15. Hammer	Transverse oblique	$(+105°, 0°, -70°)$	"A transverse projection . . . equal-area . . . based on Aitoff's projection"	Spilhaus, 1942
16. Hammer	See Appendix [37]		"Bomford's Asymmetrical Version"	Steers, 1965, p. 246

Projection	Aspect	Coordinates	Description	Reference
17. Briesemeister's modification of Hammer by shrinking eastings by 1/8	Simple (equi)oblique	(−170°, +45°, 0°)	"A new oblique equal-area projection" / "Briesemeister's Oblique Equal-area Projection of the World"	Briesemeister, 1953 / Steers, 1965, pp. 164-166 / Alitalia, 1973, pp. 2-3
18. Equidistant projection with curved radii[38]	Direct	$\Phi = +90°$, $\Lambda - \Omega = +20°$	"Modified Zenithal Equidistant Projection, Origin 0°, 160° W",39	Lewis & Campbell, 1966, pp. 14-15
19. Equidistant projection with curved radii	First transverse	(unspecified, 0°, 0°)	"Modified Zenithal"	Lewis & Campbell, 1966, pp. 6, 7, Fig. 5
20. Equidistant projection with curved radii	Second transverse	(−120°, 0°, +90°)	"Modified Zenithal Equidistant Projection, Origin 0°, 30° W",39	Lewis & Campbell, 1966, pp. 6, 12
21. Equidistant projection with curved radii	Second transverse	(+160°, 0°, −90°)	"Modified Zenithal Equidistant Projection, Origin 0°, 70° E"	Lewis & Campbell, 1966, pp. 6, 13
22. Winkel I or Eckert V	Simple oblique	(+160°, +35°, 0°)	"... the British Isles in the centre of the land areas of the world.... The projection ... might ... be called Pseudo-Cylindrical..."	Andrews, 1952
23. Littrow	Direct	$\Phi = +90°$, $\Lambda - \Omega = ±180°$	"Azimutgleichenkarte Littrow-Maurer"	Maurer, 1935, nr 189, p. 65 and plate VI
24. Littrow	First transverse	(±180°, 0°, 0°)	"Nr. 191 ist eine Umformung von Nr. 189.... Ihre Umwandlung ... bringt den Pol in die Kartenmitte"	Maurer, 1935, nr 191, p. 66
25. Littrow	Second transverse	(unspecified, 0°, +90°)	"... bilden die Haupt- und Nebenkreise des Punktpaares $\phi = 0$, $\lambda = ±90°$ ein Lambertsches Kreisnetz von der Kennzahl n = 2 ..."	Maurer, 1935, p. 65

Projection	Aspect	Aspect parameters (Λ, Φ, Ω)	Name given in reference	Reference
26. Doubly equidistant, separation 90°	Direct	$\Phi = +90°$, $\Lambda - \Omega = -150°$	"Doubly equidistant" / "Two-point equidistant"	Close, 1934 / Steers, 1965, pp. 193-194
27. Doubly equidistant, separation 39°	Transverse oblique	$(-90°, 0°, +24° \, 30')$	"A doubly equidistant projection with the pole as one point and a point of latitude 51° N. the other" / "Doubly-equidistant projection with centres A (North Pole) and B (London) 51° N."	Close, 1921 / Close, 1921
28. Doubly equidistant, separation 47° 24'	Plagal	$(+154° \, 26', +38° \, 20', +11° \, 16')$	"A doubly-equidistant projection in which the two fixed points are New York and Land's End" / "Doubly-equidistant projection of the North Atlantic Ocean: centres A (New York) 40° N., 74° W., and B (Land's End) 50° N., 6° W." / "The Two-point Equidistant Projection of the North Atlantic"	Close, 1921 / Close, 1921 / Steers, 1965, pp. 192-194
29. August	Direct	$\Phi = +90°$, $\Lambda - \Omega = $ Ferro $40 - 150°$	"Conformal Projection of the Sphere Within a two cusped Epicycloid Devised by Dr. F. August"	Deetz & Adams, 1945, p. 169 and plate VIII
30. August	Transverse oblique	$(+105°, 0°, -70°)$	"A transverse projection … based on August's projection of the sphere in a two-cusped epicycloid"	Spilhaus, 1942

31. Polyconic	Direct	$\Phi = +90°$, $\Lambda - \Omega = +80°$	"Polyconic projection"	Deetz & Adams, 1945, p. 53
32. Polyconic	Transverse oblique	$(+110°, 0°, +48°)$	"Transverse Polyconic Projection"	Deetz & Adams, 1945, p. 65 and plate II
33. Polyconic	Transverse oblique	$(+105°, 0°, +60°)$	"Transverse Polyconic Projection"	Deetz & Adams, 1945, p. 192
34. Polyconic	Transverse oblique	$(-175°, 0°, -50°)$	"The Transverse Polyconic"	Steers, 1965, pp. 121-122
35. Miller modified stereographic[41]				
— analysis (i) $\lvert m \rvert = +0.0841$	Transverse oblique	$(+110°, 0°, -72°)$	"Q . . . 0.2522 . . . centred at 18° N. and 20° E."	Miller, 1953
— analysis (ii) $-\lvert m \rvert = -0.0841$	Simple oblique	$(+160°, +72°, 0°)$		
— analysis (iii) $m = -0.0841$	Oblique	$(+160°, +72°, 0°)$		
— analysis (iv) $m = -0.0841$	Plagal[42]	See Appendix[43]		
— analysis (v) $m = -0.0841$	Oblique	$(+20°, +18°, \text{arbitrary}[44])$		
36. Cubic gnomonic	Octahedron vertex ("direct")	$\Phi = +90°$, $\Lambda - \Omega = -160°$	"Cubic Development of the Gnomonic when the Cube is tangent at the Poles and at Four Points on the Equator"	Steers, 1965, p. 50
37. Cubic gnomonic	Octahedron edge	$(+80°, +60°, 0°)$	"Projection of the sphere on the circumscribed cube"	Hinks, 1921a, pp. 43-46
			"Projection of the sphere on the circumscribed cube"	Deetz & Adams, 1945, p. 47
			"Cubic Development of the Gnomonic when the Cube is tangent at 30° N. and 100° W."	Steers, 1965, p. 51

Projection	Aspect	Aspect parameters (Λ, Φ, Ω)	Name given in reference	Reference
38. Cubic gnomonic	Octahedron edge	$(0°, +51°, 0°)$	"Projection . . . on inclined circumscribed cube"	Hinks, 1921b
39. Cubic gnomonic	Plagal	$(0°, +51°, -27°)$	"Projection . . . on oblique circumscribed cube"	Hinks, 1921b
40. Cahill octahedral	Octahedron vertex ("direct")	$\Phi = +90°,$ $\Lambda - \Omega = +157° \, 30'$	"Mr. Cahill's projection"	Geographical Journal, 1914
41. Fuller cuboctahedral	Octahedron vertex ("direct")	$\Phi = +90°,$ $\Lambda - \Omega = \pm180°$	"Fuller's Dymaxion World"	Life, 1943
42. Lee tetrahedral	Cube vertex	$(-20°, +35° \, 16', +45°)$	"Conformal tetrahedric projection"	Lee, 1965
43. Icosahedral gnomonic	Icosahedron vertex	$(+149° \, 06', +58° \, 17', 0°)$	"Polygnomonic"	Fisher, 1943, p. 618
44. Icosahedral gnomonic	Dodecahedron vertex	$(-120°, +69° \, 06', +90°)$	"Parker's flat-pole system"	Fisher, 1943, pp. 612-613
45. Icosahedral net on sphere	Dodecahedron vertex	$(-120°, +69° \, 06', +90°)$	"The polar axis passes through the centres of two opposite triangular faces, and the projection of the prime meridian is perpendicular to one side"	Hinks, 1944, p. 125

APPENDIX

The numbers of these notes correspond to the superscript numbers of the text and tables.

1. Lee's distinction between "conical" and "conic" is valuable. "Conical" includes the limiting cases where a cone becomes a plane or a cylinder; "conic" excludes these limiting cases.

2. There are actually two standard complex coordinate systems on the sphere — the one used here, for which the s plane coincides with the Mercator projection, and the Riemann-Neumann system, with complex coordinate $\sigma = e^s$, for which the σ plane coincides with the stereographic projection.

3. Maurer derives his projection nr 191 from nr 189 by a circular inversion (see [Coxeter, 1961, ch. 6] for the definition and properties of this transformation) and not by a rotation of the sphere, so he may not have been aware that these projections were two different aspects of a single projection. Maurer's "Lambertsches Kreisnetz", which he discusses in relation to both 189 and 191, is our aspect (ii).

Maurer's equations for 191 correspond, in our notation, to $z = \operatorname{csch} \bar{s}$. To convert this to our form $z = \operatorname{sech} s$ the following trivial transformations are necessary: a reflection $\bar{s} \to s$; the addition of $90°$ to all longitudes, $s \to s + \frac{1}{2} \pi i$; a rotation of the coordinate system of the z plane through $90°$.

4. A rather effective picture of a metagraticule on the sphere appears in [Robinson & Sale, 1969, p. 243].

5. Diagrams of the graticule (solid lines) superimposed on the metagraticule (broken lines) for the transverse Mercator projection appear in [Deetz & Adams, 1945, p. 123] and [Steers, 1965, p. 153]. Steers (pp. 174-175) gives an account of the significance of the metagraticule as an underlying net. His "meridians", "parallels", *projection* "latitudes" and "longitudes" (Steers's italics and quotation marks) are our metameridians, metaparallels, metalatitudes, and metalongitudes, respectively.

6. In the direct aspect, where all metameridians are meridians, we recognize the familiar notion of "central meridian".

7. Many different conventions for the Euler angles exist. The system used here is quite close to that of Jeffreys & Jeffreys [1966, pp. 108-109], whose first and third angles are $\alpha \pm 180°$ and $\gamma \pm 180°$. The most common system [Goldstein, 1959, pp. 107-109; Margenau & Murphy, 1956, pp. 286-289] takes $\alpha - 90°$ and $\gamma + 90°$ as the first and third angles.

8. *Signed* direction numbers, which are not used in this paper, differ from direction numbers in allowing negative factors of proportionality. They are intermediate in character between direction ratios and unsigned direction numbers.

9. The *near* hemisphere consists of all points with longitudes less than $90°$ east or west, the *far* hemisphere of all points with longitudes greater than $90°$. *Metanear* and *metafar* are the corresponding "meta" concepts.

10. A simple reflection in the XY or XZ planes involves only a change of sign of Φ or Ω. A reflection in the YZ plane replaces Ω by $180° - \Omega$. The trigonometric functions of Φ and Ω are left unchanged or are merely changed in sign by any of these reflections. In the columns headed "Metacoordinates Φ, Ω of pole" in Tables

3 and 4, Φ should be interpreted as Φ or $-\Phi$, and Ω as Ω, $-\Omega$, $180° + \Omega$, or $180° - \Omega$.

11. After all, an azimuthal projection, for example, centred on the south pole is just as "direct" as one centred on the north pole.

12. The north pole is chosen here for the sake of definiteness. The metacoordinates of the south pole are $(-\Phi, 180° + \Omega)$.

13. Quarter of a great circle.

14. In this paragraph, "horizontal" and "vertical" refer to the conventional orientation of the metagraticule — north is at the top in the direct aspect, hence metanorth is at the top in the general aspect.

15. Λ is here measured in radians.

16. "Circular" here includes "straight" as a special case. A straight line can be considered as a circle of infinite radius.

17. Maurer [1935, p. 52] calls the proper Lagrange graticules "die *winkeltreuen Kreisnetze erster Klasse* nach Lambert". If we consider the improper Lagrange projections (n imaginary), the singular points are at $z = \pm ik$, on the equator. See [Brown, 1935, Figures 4, 4$'$] for typical proper and improper Lagrange maps. Brown's Figure 4$'$ is a direct improper Lagrange map, *not* a second transverse proper Lagrange map.

18. Properly speaking, equation (i) with n real defines, not a plane map, but a map to a Riemann surface with branch points at $z = \pm k$. A plane map is obtained by cutting this surface from one branch point to the other to isolate a single sheet of the surface. The variable s itself is not single valued on the sphere (recall that s and $s + 2\pi i$ represent the same point on the earth); but the Riemann-Neumann coordinate $\sigma = e^s$ is single valued on the sphere and is the proper variable to be used in computing orders of branch points. If a transformation $z = f(\sigma)$ takes the sphere to a Riemann surface, and if the point $\sigma = a$ is taken into a branch point of this surface, then we define the *wedge exponent* at the point a (on the sphere) or $f(a)$ (on the surface) to be the exponent m in the approximation $z \approx A(\sigma-a)^m$ which holds in the neighbourhood of the branch point, provided $a \neq \infty$; if $a = \infty$, $1/\sigma$ is used instead of $\sigma - a$. A wedge exponent m means that a circuit of $360°$ is taken into m x $360°$ around the branch point.

19. "Standard parallel" here means "the unique straight parallel". There is no connotation of true scale. However the role of this parallel in the theory of the Lagrange projections is quite analogous to the role of the parallels of true scale in the theory of conic projections.

20. "Elliptic" and "hyperbolic" include "straight" as special cases (cf. Note 16). For the improper Von der Mühll projections the meridians are elliptic and the parallels hyperbolic, and the singularities are at $z = \pm k$, on the central meridian but not at the poles unless $n = i$. Brown [1935, Figure 5, 5$'$] shows proper and improper Von der Mühll maps. A direct improper Von der Mühll map is *not* a second transverse proper Von der Mühll map (cf. Note 17). The remarks of Notes 18 and 19 apply to the Von der Mühll projections as well as to the Lagrange projections.

21. The archetypical member of the family is Lagrange's "doubly circular projection in which Paris is the centre of least distortion, with the smallest possible increase in particular scales outward from this centre", with n and c chosen to satisfy this condition.

22. There should really be no need to apologize for "equiareal", which is, after all, a standard term in mathematics, and which has already been used to describe map projections by B.H. Brown [1935]. "Equivalent" has other useful meanings and "to saddle such a word with a technical meaning is to invite confusion" [Lenox-Conyngham, 1943-4]; "equal-area" is clumsy; "authalic" is "intolerable" [Lenox-Conyngham, 1943-4]. Lenox-Conyngham's "orthoembadic" is a long word where a shorter will do.

23. Epicycloid with two cusps.

24. MN — metanorth; similarly MS, ME, MW for the other metacardinal directions.

25. The vague phrase "shape of the fundamental region" prevents mathematical technicalities from being too obtrusive here. Technically, the number of possible aspects is equal to the number of elements in the polyhedral complex consisting of the combinatorial closure of the fundamental region. Definitions of "polyhedral complex" and "combinatorial closure" may be found in [Aleksandrov, 1956, pp. 119-120].

26. In Section 13 only five aspects were identified in analysis (iii) of the Miller modified stereographic projection. The two "missing" aspects, in which the pole has direction numbers 011 and $p11$, are not visually distinct enough from the other aspects to warrant separate consideration. The 011 aspect is equiskew, and the $p11$ aspect is derived from an oblique stereographic projection when the axis of elongation is inclined at $45°$ to the central meridian of the stereographic projection. Under analysis (iii) these two aspects are qualitatively distinct from the other aspects; they are not distinct aspects in analyses (i) or (ii); while their only peculiarity in analyses (iv) and (v) is that m is (pure) imaginary.

27. Polyhedral projections require the theory of finite groups while doubly periodic projections require discrete groups.

28. There is in fact a fourth symmetry type for polyhedral projections — *dihedral* symmetry [Coxeter, 1961, p. 282; 1973, p. 12; Fejes Tóth, 1964, p. 58; Du Val, 1964, p. 21], a *dihedron* being a polygon regarded as a degenerate regular polyhedron. The dihedral dissection of the sphere is shown in [Du Val, 1964, p. 21]. The regions mapped congruently are the lunes or gores on the sphere obtained by joining together pairs of triangles across the metequator. The fundamental regions are Du Val's triangles if the polygon has an even number of sides, and halves of his triangles if the polygon has an odd number of sides; hence the regions to be mapped congruently each contain either two or four fundamental regions. Symmetrical projections onto polygons, prisms, or other shapes having polygonal symmetry display dihedral symmetry. The Adams rhombic projection and the Petermann star projection are perhaps the best known examples of projections having dihedral symmetry.

Related symmetry types, for example *cyclic*, exist. A map with cyclic symmetry bears much the same relation to a map with dihedral symmetry as the Wiechel projection (Section 9) bears to the azimuthal projections.

29. Although we may rotate the sphere so that one of the three base points of the Chamberlin trimetric projection becomes a metapole, the irregular positions of the two other base points ensure that we have not really simplified the aspect unless the base triangle happens to be isosceles.

30. This polyhedric projection should not be confused with the polyhedral projections of Section 14. See [Steers, 1965, p. 195].

31. In an attempt to end confusion in the application of the names "Gauss-Krüger" and "Gauss-Schreiber", Lee gives rigorous mathematical definitions for these two projections in the 1961-2 paper. Unfortunately he mixes up the names himself! See [Thompson, 1971-3, p. 757] for the correct application of these names. Lee uses the name "Gauss-Krüger" correctly in his 1953-4 paper.

32. Adams gives a fifth auxiliary latitude, the *geocentric*. The corresponding auxiliary sphere, the geocentric sphere, is not an auxiliary sphere for any readily identifiable class of map projections.

33. Adams calls this the "isometric latitude". However, this name is more commonly used for a different parameter, the ψ of Section 2. The conformal latitude is the gudermannian function of the isometric latitude ψ.

34. This statement should be regarded as the basic definition of a penequidistant projection. (*Penequidistant = pene- $<$ paene*, almost, $+$ *equidistant*.) The general truly equidistant projection on the spheroid involves the calculation of lengths of spheroidal geodesics. Geodesics other than the equator and the meridians require incomplete elliptic integrals of the third kind with moduli different from the eccentricity of the spheroid. This mathematical nightmare can be avoided by using penequidistant projections as useful close approximations instead of the rigorous equidistant projections.

35. An affine transformation, consisting of a stretch in one direction, is necessary to produce perspective projections of the spheroid (except for the polar azimuthal projections) from the perspective projections of the reduced sphere. This affine transformation compensates for the polar stretching of the spheroid into the reduced sphere.

36. There is no overlap between any of these four classes of projections of the spheroid, unlike the corresponding classes of projections of the sphere. The conformal stereographic projection of the spheroid is not perspective; the perspective stereographic is not conformal. The equiareal cylindric "orthographic" projection of the spheroid is not perspective; the perspective cylindric "orthographic" is not equiareal.

37. Steers just gives the latitude, 45°N, and the longitude, 10°W, of the centre of the map and remarks that the south pole lies in the western (metawestern in our terminology) half of the map. This information is quite insufficient to decide the aspect. The best that can be done is to express Λ and Ω in terms of the unknown Φ: $\Lambda = 170° + \cos^{-1} (\tan \Phi)$, $\Omega = \cos^{-1} (\sqrt{\frac{1}{2}} \bullet \sec \Phi)$. If $\Phi = 0°$, the aspect is equioblique with $\Lambda = -100°$, $\Omega = +45°$; if $\Phi \neq 0°$, the aspect is plagal.

38. This projection is obtained from Postel's azimuthal equidistant projection by bending the radii. It is analyzed here as a doubly symmetric projection, using the conventions of Section 13. The aspect taken as direct has the radii bent towards the equator.

39. There is no indication in these names, which merely pinpoint the centres of the maps, that these two aspects are different. The second transverse aspect has the radii bent towards the central meridian.

40. The meridian of Ferro, 20° west of Paris, is taken as prime instead of Greenwich.

41. The five different analyses of this projection are listed here as separate projections. Analyses (i) and (ii) are seven-aspect analyses, (iii) is a five-aspect

analysis, while (iv) and (v) are three-aspect analyses. See Section 13 and Tables 8-10 for details. Miller's parameter $Q = -3m$.

42. "Plagal" here includes the limiting cases of simple and transverse oblique. See Table 9.

43. Any point lying on the great circle whose centre is (18°N, 20°E) may be chosen, in this particular analysis, as the metanorth metapole. The prime metameridian passes through (18°N, 20°E). If Λ is taken arbitrarily then $\Phi = -\tan^{-1} (\tan 72° \cos (\Lambda - 20°))$ and $\Omega = -\sin^{-1} (\sin 72° \sin (\Lambda - 20°))$.

44. The parameter Ω is of course completely arbitrary for a conical projection. Analysis (v) of Miller's projection has the same aspects as the stereographic.

REFERENCES

Adams, O.S. 1921. *Latitude developments connected with geodesy and cartography.* U.S. Coast and Geodetic Survey special publication 67, Washington.

Aleksandrov, P.S. 1956. *Combinatorial topology.* Vol. 1. Graylock Press, Rochester, N.Y.

Alitalia. 1973. *Route maps.* Alitalia.

Andrews, H.J. 1952. A new net for a world map. *Geographical Journal.* 118:513-514.

Arden-Close, Sir C.F. and George, F. 1952. A forgotten pseudo-zenithal projection. *Geographical Journal.* 118:237.

Bartholomew, J. ed. 1958. *The Times atlas of the world.* Mid century edition, vol. 1. The Times Publishing Company, London.

Botley, F.V. 1953-4. An octahedral gnomonic projection. *Empire Survey Review.* 12:379-381.

Bradley, A.D. 1946. Equal-area projection on the icosahedron. *Geographical Review.* 36:101-104.

Briesemeister, W. 1953. A new equal-area projection. *Geographical Review.* 43:260-261.

Brown, B.H. 1935. Conformal and equiareal world maps. *American Mathematical Monthly.* 42:212-223.

Close, Sir C.F. 1921. Note on a doubly-equidistant projection. *Geographical Journal.* 57:446-448.

————. 1929. An oblique Mollweide projection of the sphere. *Geographical Journal.* 73:251-253.

————. 1934. A doubly equidistant projection of the sphere. *Geographical Journal.* 83:144-145.

Coxeter, H.S.M. 1961. *Introduction to geometry.* John Wiley & Sons, New York.

————. 1973. *Regular polytopes.* 3rd ed. Dover Publications, New York.

Deetz, C.H. and Adams, O.S. 1945. *Elements of map projection.* 5th ed. rev. U.S. Coast and Geodetic Survey special publication 68, Washington.

Dodgson, C.L. [Lewis Carroll]. 1960. *The hunting of the Snark,* in *The humorous verse of Lewis Carroll.* Dover Publications, New York.

Du Val, P. 1964. *Homographies, quaternions, and rotations.* Clarendon Press, Oxford.

Fejes Tóth, L. 1964. *Regular figures.* Pergamon Press, Oxford.

Fisher, I. 1943. A world map on a regular icosahedron by gnomonic projection. *Geographical Review.* 33:605-619.

Gardner, M. 1961. *The second Scientific American book of mathematical puzzles and diversions.* Simon and Schuster, New York.

Geographical Journal. 1914. A new projection. *Geographical Journal.* 43:86-87.

Goldstein, H. 1959. *Classical mechanics.* 6th printing. Reading, Mass., and London.

Hall, H.D. 1948. Zones of the international frontier. *Geographical Review.* 38:615-625.

Hinks, A.R. 1921a. *Map projections.* 2nd ed. Cambridge University Press, Cambridge.

————. 1921b. The projection of the sphere on the circumscribed cube. *Geographical Journal.* 57:454-457.

————. 1941. More world maps on oblique Mercator projections. *Geographical Journal.* 97:353-356.

————. 1944. Some new effects in map projection. *Geographical Journal.* 104:123-127.

Holden, A. 1971. *Shapes, space, and symmetry.* Columbia University Press, New York and London.

Hotine, M. 1947-8. The orthomorphic projection of the spheroid — III. *Empire Survey Review.* 9:52-70.

Jackson, J.E. 1967-8. On retro-azimuthal projections. *Survey Review.* 19:319-328.

Jeffreys, Sir H. and Jeffreys, Lady Bertha. 1966. *Methods of mathematical physics.* 3rd. ed. Cambridge University Press, Cambridge.

Lee, L.P. 1943-4. The nomenclature and classification of map projections. *Empire Survey Review.* 7:190-200.

————. 1953-4. A transverse Mercator projection of the spheroid alternative to the Gauss-Krüger form. *Empire Survey Review.* 12:12-17.

————. 1961-2. The transverse Mercator projection of the entire spheroid. *Empire Survey Review.* 16:208-217.

————. 1965. Some conformal projections based on elliptic functions. *Geographical Review*. 55:563-580.

Lenox-Conyngham, Sir G.P. 1943-4. Nomenclature of map projections. *Empire Survey Review*. 7:276-278.

Lewis, Sir C. and Campbell, J.D., eds. 1966. *The Oxford Atlas,* revised reprint. Oxford University Press, London.

Life. 1943. *Life* presents R. Buckminster Fuller's dymaxion world. *Life*. 14:9 41-55.

Margenau, H. and Murphy, G.M. 1956. *The mathematics of physics and chemistry,* 2nd ed. D. Van Nostrand Company, Princeton, N.J.

Maurer, H. 1935. *Ebene Kugelbilder, ein Linnésches System der Kartenentwürfe.* Supplement 221 to *Petermanns Mitteilungen.* Justus Perthes, Gotha.

Miller, O.M. 1953. A new conformal projection for Europe and Asia. *Geographical Review*. 43:405-409.

Reignier, F. 1957. *Les systèmes de projection et leurs applications à la géographie, à la cartographie, à la navigation, à la topometrie, etc....* Vol. I. L'Institut Géographique National, Paris.

Robinson, A.H. and Sale, R.D. 1969. *Elements of cartography.* 3rd ed. John Wiley & Sons, New York.

Spilhaus, A.F. 1942. Maps of the whole world ocean. *Geographical Review*. 32:431-435.

Steers, J.A. 1965. *An introduction to the study of map projections.* 14th ed. University of London Press, London.

Thompson, E.H. 1971-3. Coordinate systems and map projections. [Book review.] *Photogrammetric Record*. 7:755-758.

General Information

Each monograph in this series will cover one aspect of cartography and will comprise either a single major work, or a collection of research papers relevant to a principal theme.

Subjects to be chosen for the monographs will include the many topics that comprise cartography, e.g. the history and development of cartography, topographic and thematic mapping, analysis of national and regional atlases, the techniques of map production, automation in cartography, map design, map projections and map librarianship.

This series of monographs complements *The Canadian Cartographer*.

Subscriptions

Subscriptions may be entered on an annual or standing order basis for *Cartographica*. The subscription rate is $12.00 for the three monographs. Single copies are $4.00 each. Orders may be placed direct with the publisher or through any agency.
The monographs may be ordered as supplements to *Canadian Cartographer* at a combined subscription rate of $15.00 for 5 issues (2 numbers of *Canadian Cartographer* and 3 monographs per year).

Address enquiries to:

General Editor, Department of Geography, York University
4700 Keele Street, Toronto, Canada
Executive Secretary: Thora H. Tuckett, Geography, York University, Toronto

CARTOGRAPHICA

DESIGNED AND
COMPOSED BY THE PUBLICATIONS OFFICE
YORK UNIVERSITY
TEXT IN 11 ON 15 BASKERVILLE MEDIUM
PRINTED ON ZEPHYR ANTIQUE BY
THE UNIVERSITY OF TORONTO PRESS